Emotional Life

Managing your feelings to make
the most of your precious time on Earth

Emotional Life

Managing your feelings to make
the most of your precious time on Earth

Dr Doreen Davy

**PSYCHE
BOOKS**

Winchester, UK
Washington, USA

First published by Psyche Books, 2014
Psyche Books is an imprint of John Hunt Publishing Ltd., Laurel House, Station Approach,
Alresford, Hants, SO24 9JH, UK
office1@jhpbooks.net
www.johnhuntpublishing.com
www.psyche-books.com

For distributor details and how to order please visit the 'Ordering' section on our website.

ISBN: 978 1 78279 276 5

A CIP catalogue record for this book is available from the British Library.

Design: Lee Nash

Printed and bound by CPI Group (UK) Ltd, Croydon, CR0 4YY

We operate a distinctive and ethical publishing philosophy in all
areas of our business, from our global network of authors to
production and worldwide distribution.

CONTENTS

Introduction

I decided to write this book because I want people to understand just how powerful emotions are and why they are such an integral part of being human. I know from my own experiences (based on my professional and personal life) that emotions are incredibly powerful. However, I also know that it's possible to master and use that special power in order to live a happy, healthy and fulfilling life, which is mainly what this book is all about.

As a practicing psychologist, my job is to help unhappy people to feel better. Given the knowledge I have gained over the years in regard to human happiness and misery, I believe I am well qualified to provide you the reader, with valuable guidance on the subject of emotions. During my time as a psychologist, I have helped thousands of people to feel better by teaching them skills and strategies that place them in the 'driver's seat' of their emotional life.

As well as teaching skills and strategies for managing emotions, this book contains a philosophical thread that weaves its way throughout, hopefully providing you with an inspirational experience that will make a lasting and positive difference to how you view your emotions and how you live your life. As you read through the book, you will be finding out how emotions can positively or negatively affect many important areas of your life, such as relationships, health, communication, behaviour, authenticity, goals, philosophy and spirituality.

Experiencing strong positive feelings not only creates blissful moments that enhance your life, these types of emotions are also good for your health. How to experience these valuable emotions on a daily basis is covered early on in the book. Chapters on meditation and mindfulness techniques are included as being ways in which you can further experience powerful emotions.

These exercises can be learned by anybody, and when practiced regularly, the benefits are considerable.

We will also be looking at negative emotions, where they come from and the mental, physical and behavioural damage they can cause. Examples taken from everyday situations will help you to quickly recognise how easily negative emotions can escalate out of control, and a variety of useful strategies are provided that can prevent this from happening. By the time you have finished reading the book, you will have a far greater understanding of emotions (your own as well as those of other people), enabling you to really start making the most of your precious time on Earth. Many of the examples in the book are based on common problems that clients have presented with over the years. To protect clients' confidentiality, pseudonyms are used throughout and identifying details have been altered. The terms 'partner' and 'spouse' are used interchangeably for ease of reading.

I have always had an interest in psychology. Even in previous occupational roles such as office administrator, retail assistant, trainer and manager, and the more general roles as wife, mother, daughter, sister and friend, I have always found people to be fascinating. From watching how customers choose their purchases to observing the obsequious behaviour of lower-level managers at business meetings, human psychology seems always to have been my main focus.

I'm probably not a typical psychologist, having been born and raised in a working-class area of Liverpool in North-West England, a place where life opportunities (at that time) were limited. Any ideas of going to university or having a career were never even considered as possibilities. Like many young women in Liverpool during the late 1960s, I was eager to get married, and so at the age of sixteen I became engaged, and married two years later. By the time I was twenty-five I had emigrated to the other side of the world with my husband and two young children. New Zealand is a beautiful country and has been my home for a long time now. In many ways life has not been easy, but being raised in Liverpool provided me with a quirky way of looking at life, and that special Liverpudlian brand of humour that encourages people to laugh at themselves.

While continuing to work, I gained a tertiary education at Massey University in Palmerston North and Auckland, completing a Bachelor of Arts in English Literature, two Graduate Diplomas (one in Business Studies and one in Psychology), a Masters Degree with First Class Honours in Psychology (for which I was awarded a Doctoral Scholarship) and finally a PhD in Psychology. The latter qualifications provided me with the opportunity to register and work as a psychologist. At the Auckland Institute for Cognitive and Behaviour Therapies, I completed a final Graduate Diploma in CBT, this being the particular therapeutic approach I mostly use in my work. Cognitive therapy is about how we think, behaviour therapy is about what we do, and the combination of these two psychotherapies – cognitive behaviour therapy (commonly referred to as CBT) – has produced one of the most successful therapeutic treatments in use today.

As the focus of the book is human emotions, I have included some of my own personal experiences to share with you. My aim is to provide you with strategies and skills that will help you to become the master of your own emotions. My hope is that the philosophical thread running throughout the book will provide you with a sense of awe and wonder as you fully appreciate the opportunity you have been given to take part in the greatest and most mysterious adventure of all – *your* life.

Chapter One

Understanding Emotions

I don't want to be at the mercy of my emotions, I want to use them, to enjoy them, and to dominate them.
Oscar Wilde

Emotions are powerful. They are able to wreak havoc or create bliss across the full spectrum of our lives. In this first chapter of the book, I want to introduce you to different types of emotions, the effects they have on our bodies and how they influence our behaviour. Not only is it important to understand what emotions are and where they come from, we need to be able to harness their special power in order to live happy and healthy lives.

If unhelpful negative emotions are stopping you from making the most of your life, the good news is that you *can* do something about it. If positive uplifting emotions are not part of your everyday experience, then some more good news – you can definitely do something about that too. Once you understand how your own emotions impact on your experience of life, you can begin to gain mastery over them. Then, with your emotions directly under your control by maximising positive emotions and minimising negative emotions, it becomes easy to make the most of every single day of your life.

What Are Emotions?

The first step towards achieving emotional mastery is to understand what emotions are. The word emotion comes from the Latin *emovere* which means 'to move', suggesting that emotions are able to move us in some way. Positive emotions such as happiness, love and joy obviously move us in ways that make us feel good whereas negative emotions such as jealousy, anger or hate move us towards feeling unhappy.

Over 2000 years ago, the Greek philosopher Aristotle noted that emotions "may be felt both too much and too little, and in both cases not well." In our modern times, it seems that little has changed. You have probably heard some people labelled by others as being 'emotional', implying that they are a bit 'flaky', a bit over the top in their emotional responses. Alternatively, others might be described as 'unemotional', a term also having negative connotations, the implication here being that the person is lacking in empathy, openness or understanding of others, a bit like the character Mr Spock from the TV series *Star Trek*. When there are too many negative emotions and too few positive emotions being experienced, the result is usually a miserable and unhealthy life. The opposite of this – plenty of positive emotions and very few negative emotions – usually ensures a healthy and happy life, which is the main focus of this book.

Different Types of Emotions

How much we enjoy our lives or how miserable we feel is largely determined by our emotional state. Do you recognise when you are feeling emotionally charged, whether it's a negative or positive experience? Could you give a name to the different types of emotions you might experience? Let's look at a few examples of emotions starting with those that provide positive experiences. These are: loving, happy, joyful, enthusiastic, exhilarated, playful, inspired, pleased, grateful, relaxed, content, serene, peaceful, enchanted, proud, hopeful, reassured and relieved. These are the types of emotions that are good to experience as much as possible in our lives. A lack of positive emotions can leave us with a sense of boredom and indifference. We become passionless people, having a vague feeling that life should be happier but with few ideas about how to achieve this.

Now let's look at some emotions that most of us would probably prefer to experience as little as possible. Examples of negative emotions are: angry, bitter, lonely, discouraged, rejected, ashamed, worthless, resentful, offended, jealous, hopeless, depressed, terrified, anxious, pressured, guilty, distressed, heart-broken, threatened and disgusted.

Emotions such as compassion or sympathy could be described as being positive or negative. For example, compassion could be regarded as a good civilising emotion, yet the person feeling compassionate might describe it as an unpleasant negative experience because she is watching the suffering of another.

'Healthy' Versus Unhealthy Negative Emotions

Emotions are such a key part of being human, it pays to not only recognise and understand them, but to also have control over them, especially those emotions capable of causing real suffering. One of the ways we can do this is by making sure that our emotional response is appropriate to the situation. From my observations as a psychologist, much of the emotional suffering that people experience is totally unnecessary, and is often because the intensity of what they are feeling doesn't equate with the situation.

Plenty of situations in life are frustrating, for example, working alongside difficult people or when things don't go the way we expect them to, so it's quite normal to experience low-level negative emotions. These are referred to as *healthy* negative emotions, not because they are good for us but because it's normal and healthy to experience them now and again. Unfortunately, we can sometimes let these mild negative emotions quickly become *unhealthy* extreme negative emotions, which is where the real suffering awaits. Here are some examples:

Situation – Stuck in a Traffic Jam
Healthy Negative Emotion – Frustration
Unhealthy Negative Emotion – Rage

Situation – Pet Dies
Healthy Negative Emotion – Sadness
Unhealthy Negative Emotion – Depression

Situation – Misplaced Keys
Healthy Negative Emotion – Concern
Unhealthy Negative Emotion – Panic

Situation – Missed Out on Job Application
Healthy Negative Emotion – Disappointment
Unhealthy Negative Emotion – Despair

Situation – Spilt Drink at a Party
Healthy Negative Emotion – Embarrassment
Unhealthy Negative Emotion – Shame

Situation – Made a Mistake at Work
Healthy Negative Emotion – Regret
Unhealthy Negative Emotion – Guilt

Do you recall any times when your negative emotional response didn't match the situation? Obviously, the more extreme the negative response, the worse we feel. As everyday life can involve a variety of situations capable of triggering negative feelings, it's essential to know the difference between a balanced healthy reaction and an unbalanced extreme reaction if you want to avoid unnecessary suffering. Fortunately, there are strategies you can learn to help ensure that the emotional response matches the situation. These useful strategies are fully covered a little later on in Chapter Six.

Emotions and Gender Differences
Over the years in my work, I have noticed a lot of male clients complain about how 'emotional' their female partners are. Some

men obviously feel quite confused by women's emotional responses, attributing this to stress, hormones or simply something associated with being female. Interestingly, it's also fairly common for female clients to complain that their male partners are emotionally 'closed off' because of their reluctance to physically demonstrate or verbally express their feelings.

Generally, females are more expressive and in tune with their own and others' emotional states than are males. This isn't surprising as neurological research shows that females tend to have more active neurons in the left hemisphere of their brains (a part associated with language) than males. In addition, the bridge that connects the right and left hemispheres of the brain is often stronger in females than in males, allowing females to more easily process information from both sides of the brain. These findings help to explain why, on average, females are more emotionally aware and expressive than males.

Men are emotional beings too of course, and they experience the same smorgasbord of feelings that women do, but a lot of males do seem to find it difficult to verbalise how they are feeling emotionally, preferring to use expressions such as 'uncomfortable', 'okay' or 'really good' rather than more specific descriptions. This may partly be attributed to culturally learned behaviour given that throughout history males have been suppressing many of their feelings in order to appear 'manly'. Even now, boys crying or showing fear in front of others in the schoolyard can still be regarded as being 'girly'. Because of this learned behaviour combined with a lack of practice in expressing emotions, some men avoid talking about how they feel, the consequence of this being a lack of real connection with others.

The fact that females are generally more emotionally aware than males may help to explain why female warfare in the schoolyard often involves hurting other girls at a direct emotional level. This is usually via exclusion or verbal put-downs, whereas schoolyard warfare amongst boys is generally more physical – shoving, kicking, and punching – although this indirectly brings emotional hurt as well.

The Impact of Emotions on Physiology and Behaviour

Even if we can't put a name to the specific emotion being felt, we experience it at a physical level. Emotions are so powerful, they create changes in the biochemistry of our bodies which can be physically harmful or beneficial depending upon the type of emotion being experienced. This is why emotions are capable of providing that extra energy boost described as passion or an adrenalin rush to enhance a performance or activity. The singer who is experiencing her song at an emotional level while performing seems to sing better. Sometimes it can be as though the emotion is contagious as the audience experiences it too. Strong emotion can also provide that extra energy for athletes, helping them to perform at their very best.

There was an article in a local newspaper recently describing how an ordinary everyday person experienced such a surge of adrenalin that he had the strength to lift the weight of a car to help free his brother who was trapped underneath. We have probably all heard of miraculous feats of strength or endurance that occur when people are faced with a crisis. These heroes often wonder afterwards how they managed to perform as they did, for example, fighting off wild animals or lifting heavy objects they couldn't otherwise move. The strong emotion experienced at the time of the crisis would not only have affected their physiology but also their focus and determination to try and do whatever is needed to save themselves or others.

Although not in the same category, I know from personal experience that my emotions can provide the motivation I need to keep exercising when I'm more than ready to quit. When I start pedalling on my exercise cycle at home, it seems like really hard work and pretty soon my legs feel like jelly and my knees are hurting, and that's when it's very easy to climb off the bike and head for the kitchen to make a cup of tea, do some ironing or anything! But I have found that the type of music playing while I pedal can make a huge difference. As an example, just the other day I was about to quit after only forty calories' worth of exercise when Frank Sinatra singing 'New York, New York' started playing. Totally engaged in listening to this music, I was suddenly full of emotional and physical energy. For whatever the reason, this old song seemed to connect with me emotionally. The cycling changed from being a chore to a joyful experience, and when the song finished I had totted up an extra thirty calories on the cycle meter! So what was happening here? The music had a positive emotional influence on me which affected my body, filling me with a 'happy energy'. As emotions can have a significant impact on what we do and how we do it, it probably comes as no surprise to learn that music and emotions are closely connected – a fascinating subject we will be looking at in the following chapter.

Body Language

Emotions can be difficult to hide as they tend to manifest in our bodies and communicate on our behalf. This well-known phenomenon is referred to as body language. As an example, professional card players often closely observe the body language of their opponents. A shift in body posture, pupil dilation or minute facial flickers can reveal the true emotional state of a person, and perhaps provide some clues as to what cards others are holding.

Although we may be saying nothing, or perhaps even attempting to portray an opposite emotion, our real emotions are conveyed through our bodies. For example, if you are upset by somebody's rude remark towards you at a social event, no matter how hard you try to pretend otherwise, your body language and your tone of voice are likely to communicate the hurt you are feeling. If you feel secretly attracted to another person, your

7

body will inadvertently speak up on your behalf. Whether the other person picks up your body's signals will depend on how emotionally aware they are.

Biological Changes

Biological changes caused by emotions can have a direct impact on our health and longevity. Research has shown that the immune system is significantly strengthened when we experience positive emotions, leaving us better able to ward off disease and even reduces the risk of strokes and heart attacks.

Conversely, experiencing negative emotions is associated with harmful physical consequences. When we experience strong negative emotions, complex changes take place in our bodies as stress hormones are released into the blood stream. The human body is well equipped to cope with occasional negative emotions and quickly recover, however, if we experience these types of feelings on a long-term basis, the effect on our bodies can be harmful, lowering the quality of our sleep, weakening the immune system and leaving us more vulnerable to illness. Not surprisingly, happier, more optimistic people tend to be healthier and live longer than those with a more negative view of life.

Although we may be largely unaware of the biological changes taking place in our bodies when we experience strong emotions, there are direct physical changes also taking place, changes we are fully aware of. Let's now look at how some emotions can impact at a very direct level on our bodies.

Anxious

When anxious, we are usually aware of feeling hot or trembling. Our breathing may become fast and shallow and our heart rate accelerates. Anxiety is usually associated with a sense of threat, so when we feel anxious, the sympathetic nervous system triggers the 'fight or flight' response. To fight or to flee is our built-in physical survival mechanism which developed to help our early ancestors when they were in dangerous situations. Anxiety is one of the most common emotions that people experience and is covered more fully in Chapter Four.

Angry

Anger is an energising emotion, and like jealousy, envy and resentment, it is usually associated with a sense of something being unfair. In its extreme form (rage and fury), anger can be a destructive force, temporarily causing a loss of control combined with a strong desire to hurt someone or destroy something. When we start to become angry, a feeling of tension rises which surges through the body creating an urge to take action or respond in some physical way – to squeeze, hit, throw, jump, spit, kick or even to bite. I once witnessed someone 'hopping mad'. This person was literally hopping from one foot to the other as the energy of their anger released itself in this way. More commonly though, anger finds an outlet through our dialogue, prompting us to swear, yell or make hurtful remarks that we can later regret.

Although anger is largely viewed as a 'bad' emotion, there are situations when it can be very useful. Without the energy of collective anger directed towards societal change, atrocities such as slavery, live burnings, rape and the torture of people and animals might still be a regular occurrence. In the right situation, a boost of anger can be of great benefit. For example, seeing somebody kicking a dog or harming a child would probably make most of us feel outraged, which in turn would create a rush of energy towards stopping the brutality. So we could say that anger in the right context is beneficial to society.

As well as being roused by a one-off situation, anger can build up from accumulated stresses. When the latest stressor becomes 'the straw that broke the camel's back', the consequence can be an outburst of anger. Fortunately, most of us are able to control our anger impulses, especially when we are in settings where it would be inappropriate such as at work or in public areas. Once home though, and out of society's view, the meekest of people can 'explode', allowing the release of pent-up anger to impact on their relationships with others. Pent-up anger is not good for us physically or mentally. It's far better that we speak up for ourselves in an assertive way when we need to, rather than allow a build-up of this mostly damaging emotion.

Sad

Think for a moment about what it's like to experience the emotion of sadness. Tears may come easily, you feel a lump in your throat, and your body might feel sluggish, heavy and tired. And when we are physically tired, other feelings such as irritability and boredom are heightened. Sadness can also affect sleeping patterns, libido and appetite. A low mood brought on by grief or a bout of depression is often associated with a sense of loss. It may be the loss of a family member or friend, the end of a relationship, redundancy, health problems or even moving house. I have seen clients who become very down when their pets die, immigrants grieving for their homeland or mothers suffering the pangs of Empty Nest Syndrome when their last child leaves home – all situations connected with loss.

We all feel sad now and again and this is quite normal. However, if you feel as though you have become 'stuck' in a feeling of sadness that isn't lifting and has been around for weeks or months rather than days, then it may be a case of clinical depression or a symptom of some other health-related problem. Either way, a visit to your medical doctor may be warranted.

Happy

Having looked briefly at three negative emotions (anxiety, anger and sadness), let's now look at the main positive emotion – happiness. Feeling happy is an emotionally healthy state. It creates a positive liveliness and a pleasant feeling that most of us would probably like to experience as part of our everyday life. This emotion has an upbeat energy, providing confidence so that obstacles or difficulties are faced rather than avoided. This in turn helps to develop resilience and problem solving abilities, all of which contribute to better life experiences.

Recent research has shown that happiness can be contagious. Simply being in the presence of happy optimistic people can have a favourable impact on our own emotional state. See if you notice this happening next time you interact socially. You may notice how certain individuals can bolster the spirits of those around them, their upbeat happy energy having a positive influence on people. When we feel happy, we tend to be more interested and aware of what's going on around us, we are more spontaneous, open and playful, we tend to laugh more easily, and having a good hearty laugh can do wonders as an internal workout for the body. In short, it makes good sense to aim to be as happy as you can.

Using Emotions

What purpose is there in us having emotions? Why did we evolve to have such powerful feelings capable of causing so much pleasure or suffering? These are the questions that people sometimes ask during their therapy sessions. The answer is that we developed emotions because they are of key importance to our survival. Positive emotions such as love can bond us strongly together as a family or community, improving our chances of survival because there is more efficiency as well as safety in numbers. Feeling happy has good survival value as it enhances the appetite for food and sex as well as providing energy and motivation to get going on tasks. Other emotions such as fear and anger can be valuable for defence purposes, providing protection from threat for the more vulnerable members of a community.

Emotions such as patriotic pride, guilt or shame can be useful for maintaining social order and conformity. For instance, during the First World War in England, men who refused to fight in the armed forces were often given white feathers by women, the intention of this being to publicly shame them as cowards. I wonder sometimes, when watching television documentaries showing the horror of the trenches, how many young men fought and died in that seemingly senseless war solely to avoid being shamed as cowards by their own English society. My guess is quite a few.

Emotional Memory Exercise

Emotions can also be used as a way of making sure we remember something important. When there is a strong emotional element to remembering something, then it's harder to forget. As a way of demonstrating this, you could try the following exercises. Have somebody create a secret list of any ten items (for example, hairbrush, car, elastic band, kettle, and so on) and then the person who made up the list reads the items out aloud with a few seconds of silence between each one. Once the last item has been read out, you have to try and remember as many as possible, naming the items in any order, but all within a one-minute timeframe.

Now do the same exercise again (using ten different items), but this time create a story in your mind beforehand that adds an element of emotion. For example, think of a person you dearly love and imagine he or she is a castaway, marooned and alone on a desert island. Every item you remember will be given to your loved one to help in their effort to survive (when marooned on an island, even an elastic band can be valuable!). Don't let the person creating the list of items know you are thinking in this way. Adding a story with an emotional element to it changes the exercise from being just a memory game to something important that will help your loved one survive. Notice how many more items you can remember when emotions are involved compared to the first time when it was just a basic word memory game.

When I do this second exercise, I remember every item because strong emotions such as love and caring become involved, which make it important that I don't forget. Making up a story from a random list of words adds 'meaning', making it easier for us to remember, but adding a strong emotional element can make the story even more memorable.

Emotions and Exploitation

Writer Stephen Butler Leacock described advertising as – "the science of arresting the human intelligence long enough to get money out of it." We now have commercial messages dominating almost every aspect of life. Flicking through magazines and newspapers recently, I noticed there are certain images being widely used to depict 'happiness' and 'lifestyle'. These involve smiling attractive people holding glasses of wine, usually set against a pleasant background. It may be a group of friends or perhaps a couple in a spa-pool, all with glasses of wine raised in celebration. Even in advertisements for retirement homes there are now images of happy people (a bit older but still attractive and smiling), clinking glasses with their friends while sharing the ubiquitous bottle of wine. It seems as though the glass of wine has come to symbolise 'good times' as most of these products or services being advertised have nothing to do with selling alcohol.

These types of images are commonly used in advertisements to manipulate us at an emotional level. Their aim is to help us associate feeling good with a particular product or service. Have you ever noticed how often music is played in the background of advertisements on TV? The people who create these commercials understand the enormous influence that music can have on our emotions. I remember many years ago sitting at home watching TV with my sisters when a commercial appeared showing a beautiful woman unwrapping and eating a chocolate bar. As she slowly and rapturously enjoyed each bite, Mozart's exquisite

'Elvira Madigan' (from Piano Concerto 21) played in the background. This powerful visual and aural assault on our senses had us immediately rushing off to buy some 'chocolate bliss' at the local shop! Advertising creators know that the fastest way to opening a customer's purse is via the emotions.

As well as showing us how we can feel good, advertising personnel understand people's desire for approval and acceptance by others, and often use this as an emotional angle to sell their products. They demonstrate how easy it is to find an attractive partner if we use a certain type of deodorant or toothpaste, or by simply driving the right type of car we can become the envy of everybody around us. As consumers, it's often our emotions that determine what we buy, and the more these images are flashed about on billboards, the internet, TV, magazines and newspapers, the more we begin to develop ideas about what it is we 'need' to have. It seems as though the aim of the marketing industry is to create more and more consumers with insatiable acquisitive desires.

This is not to say we can't find pleasure in enjoying wine with friends or we can't enjoy driving a flashy new car, but there is a difference between being authentic (choosing what you really want) and merely responding to the mindless consumerism encouraged by advertisements. It's easy to allow ourselves to be conditioned into believing that life would be so much better if only we had these 'things', and that by not having them we are somehow missing out.

Making your own authentic lifestyle choices places you in the 'driver's seat' of your emotional life. When you are fully engaged in making the most of really 'being here', it provides a freedom for *you* to choose how you want to live your precious allotted bit of time on Earth. To experience powerful positive emotions as a result of doing what you really want to do is far more rewarding than simply responding to the superficial offerings of the marketing and advertising industries.

To help you to achieve this, the following chapter looks at how we can create valuable positive emotions that are able to lift our spirits in a special kind of way.

This above all: to thine own self be true.
William Shakespeare

Chapter Two

Creating Positive Emotions

The very purpose of our life is happiness.
Dalai Lama

There are some people who advise us to not even bother pursuing happiness, that if it happens to turn up in life, then enjoy it, but don't go seeking it out. From my perspective this couldn't be more wrong. Taking such a passive approach to your life is not 'making the most of it'. Experiencing positive emotions is what happiness is all about and although we may not have full control over every situation in life, we can take quite a lot of responsibility for our personal level of happiness by consciously choosing to engage in activities that will enrich our lives.

Defining Happiness

As part of the American Declaration of Independence, Thomas Jefferson declared that "Life, liberty and the pursuit of happiness" is an "inalienable human right." But what is happiness and how do we go about pursuing it? We know it is a positive emotion but if somebody asked you right now – "are you happy?" – what would you say? Can people be in a continual state of happiness or is it a feeling we experience now and again? Or is being 'happy enough' as much as we can hope for?

There are different forms of happiness. Strong positive feelings such as joy, awe, bliss, delight and rapture tend to be fleeting and of a temporary nature, while gentler forms of happiness such as contentment, gratitude, serenity and pleasure are experienced at a lower level but over a longer period of time. To my mind, happiness is a state that can be experienced as a general background feeling, whereas a strong fleeting emotion such as joy is heart-lifting in the fullest sense of the word. Experiencing joy is easily recognisable because we feel it at a physical level, we know we have been emotionally moved.

Hedonism

Superficial pleasure-seeking is often referred to as hedonism. A hedonist is typically thought of as somebody who pursues self-indulgence, often in the form of physical pleasures involving food, drink and sex. You could say there's nothing wrong with being a hedonist and that it's a much better approach to life than puritanical self-denial. I believe a little hedonism is healthy and, in the words of the old music-hall song, "A little of what you fancy does you good." To provide an example, there's something extremely pleasurable about lying down on the sofa after a weekend lunch, and slowly savouring a smallish to medium-sized bar of chocolate (even without Mozart playing in the background!). Although this is a thoroughly enjoyable experience at a physical level, it doesn't provide the uplifting heartfelt emotions that other activities can, and if I were to partake of this chocolate delight on a daily basis, it would simply become a habit, and I prefer to develop habits that are good for me. But now and again, a bit of chocolate-flavoured hedonism is very nice!

In Pursuit of Sublime Moments

If we are to take responsibility for our personal happiness, then we need to become masters of our emotions. As well as minimising negative feelings, it's important that we make a concerted effort to increase positive emotional experiences. I'm not referring here to basic pleasures or quick-fix highs involving drugs or alcohol, but rather engaging in activities that can provide 'sublime moments' – those powerful emotions such as a deep feeling of bliss or a profound sense of awe or wonder – emotions that are able to 'move the heart'.

In order to experience sublime moments in life, you need to be aware of your own 'emotional barometer' and the types of activities or situations that can provide strong positive feelings for you. In other words, you need to recognise when you are experiencing these emotions and be aware of what you are actually doing at that time. We are all influenced by different things based on our unique personalities and life experiences, so activities capable of creating these strong positive emotions obviously won't be the same for everyone.

For some, physical exercise can create a joyful experience – running is well known for providing a 'jogger's high'. For others, it could be dancing, singing or listening to music. Engaging in sports-related activities such as surfing, sailing or skiing commonly provides a sense of exhilaration. Whatever activities have the power to lift your spirits, direct your focus and energy in that direction.

Seeking Beauty

If you are not sure what could create sublime moments for you, then a good place to start is with the concept of beauty. There is the well-known saying – "Beauty is in the eye of the beholder" – meaning that beauty is subjective, we each have our own idea of what is beautiful. Try this little exercise for a day: simply be open to observing what might (to you) be beautiful. You will be amazed at what you discover about yourself and the world around you. Becoming a seeker and observer of beauty is highly rewarding. Not only does it provide useful insights into who we are at a very personal level, it offers delightful moments to savour on a daily basis.

In her poem *Aurora Leigh*, Elizabeth Barrett Browning described Earth as being "crammed with heaven." And she is right. When we start really looking, beauty is everywhere, accessible via our physical senses. For example, we can see beauty in nature (lakes, trees, mountains, the sunrise and sunset), and we can hear beauty in music. Some may even taste beauty or certainly an intense pleasure (chocolate comes to mind again here!). The smell of perfumes, incense or flowers can be beautiful and we can touch beauty in objects of art (fine china, glass or marble). The soft skin of a baby or the fur of an animal can also feel beautiful. I remember once touching the skin of a snake and found it to be a surprisingly delightful sensation, like touching the most exquisite silk. The world really is brimming over with beauty, so try becoming a seeker of beauty and by encountering your own particular forms of beauty, you will experience more moments of pleasure, happiness and perhaps even the sublime on a daily basis.

People who surround themselves with beautiful objects and who love the sight or the feel of these objects will understand the words from the first line of Keats' poem *Endymion:* "A thing of beauty is a joy forever." Because beauty is so subjective, you need to make your own discoveries based on your own emotional responses. For some, science is beautiful. Marie Curie, the famous scientist who discovered radium once said "I am among those who think that science has great beauty." Another of the same opinion was one of the world's most famous scientists – Albert Einstein. In the quote below, Einstein describes the sense of awe he experienced when exploring the mysteries that lay within the realm of physics.

The most beautiful emotion we can experience is the mysterious. It is the fundamental emotion that stands at the cradle of all true art and science. He to whom this emotion is a stranger, who can no longer wonder and stand rapt in awe, is as good as dead, a snuffed-out candle.
Albert Einstein

For me, there are many activities or situations that comprise an element of beauty, sometimes even leading to the sublime. Given their ability to create powerful emotional experiences, I have selected a few of them to share with you in this chapter. Most belong in my 'happiness' category and all have at times triggered an intense emotional response. My aim here is to provide you with some examples (which may or may not resonate with you) that for me are able to create strong positive emotions. By continuing to leave myself open to new experiences, I hope to add to my special happiness list as I journey through life.

Music

More than almost anything else, music has the ability to create strong emotions that transport me to what seems to be another dimension, a rapturous state. It can be an experience that has a powerful effect on my whole being. Emotional heights can be reached when that feeling of 'being at one' with music occurs and, unlike taking drugs or alcohol, there are no negative consequences.

These feelings of rapture are sometimes brought about by a familiar song that happens to be playing at the right time, creating a strong emotional connection. Although my tastes are eclectic, there are certain pieces of music that create a powerful appreciation of aural beauty. A few examples would be: Tchaikovsky's Piano Concerto Number 1, 'The Kyrie' from Mozart's Great Mass in C minor and Bruch's Violin Concerto Number 1. When listening to these classical masterpieces, I feel proud to be a human being and wonder what any highly-evolved aliens might conclude on listening to such music. Perhaps they would marvel at how such a primitive species could create so much beauty!

Then of course, there is opera. What music can be more emotional than operatic arias? Some of these have created great emotional highs for me and probably for millions of other people too. A few examples of many include: 'Che Gilida Manina' from *La Boheme* by Puccini; 'Within the Holy Temple' from *The Pearl*

Fishers by Bizet; 'Soave Sia Il Vento' from *Cosi Fan Tutte* by Mozart, and 'O, Silver Moon' from *Rusalka* by Dvorak.

In order to really appreciate sublime musical experiences, I have found it best to listen with closed eyes, focusing the mind solely on the sound of the music. Sometimes, when I'm in the car next to my husband who is driving, as the certain piece of music playing is approaching the 'climax' (which is often where the sublime moment awaits), he will alert me to some mundane fact such as "Look, they're building another McDonalds over there." Breaking from the musical revelry, I wonder how he can be so oblivious to what I'm experiencing as he can hear the music too. Sometimes I don't respond at all to his comments, I keep my eyes closed and simply put my hand up to signal DO NOT DISTURB, SUBLIME MOMENT IN PROGRESS!

There's a distinction between what I call sublime music and music that is simply pleasurable, but I believe both types nourish mind, body and 'soul'. Even if there's no such thing as a soul, music makes you feel as though there is. I remember a couple of years ago, it was my mother's 90th birthday, and our family organised a special little party for her. She is quite frail and afraid of falling, so she sat and tapped her hands and feet to the music we organised for her, which included her favourite songs from during the war period, Viennese waltzes and even Irish jigs. But on that day there was only one particular song that managed to get her up dancing (something she had always loved to do). It was 'Begin the Beguine' sung almost completely in Spanish by Julio Iglesias. She loved his sexy voice and the rhythm of the music, even though she hardly understood a word of the song! Her fear of falling seemed to vanish as she moved her frail old body to the music. If there really is such a thing as a soul, then it's at times like these when the soul is 'touched'. Watching my mother dancing once more to Julio's music, seeing the expression of bliss on her face, and with my sisters and I all swaying along next to her, this was one of my life's highlights.

Music can raise the spirits very quickly, especially when the songs are old familiar favourites. For me, such songs provide poignant feelings, often bringing a tearful joy.

In my work I sometimes need to drive to clients' homes to see them as a few are unable to get out because of injuries. Turning on the local radio station while I drive and listening to some of the songs being played is like catching up with old well-loved friends. Some of these songs can immediately trigger a strong emotional impact, pulling at the heartstrings and creating emotional energy. Here are just a few of my most beloved of 'old friends': 'The Power of Love' by Jennifer Rush; 'Una Paloma Blanca' by George Baker Selection (this song creates instant happiness!); 'That's Amore' by Dean Martin; 'Good Morning Starshine' by Oliver (I used to sing this song to my firstborn when he woke me up in the mornings. I would lift him out of his cot and dance around the bedroom with him in my arms while I sang!); 'Love Changes Everything' by Michael Ball and 'Goodbye My Love Goodbye' by Demis Roussos. I could go on naming hundreds of songs here, but I'm sure you could produce your own list according to your own emotional experiences.

Research has shown that listening to music we like produces increased levels of dopamine in the brain's nucleus accumbens, which create a feeling of being 'high'. Music can have such a powerful emotional impact on us, it directly (as well as indirectly) affects our physiology. As an example, some years ago I was invited to a party by a friend, but because I had a migraine at the time, I didn't feel well enough to go. But I really *did* want to go, so by way of a compromise I decided to go, but only stay for half an hour. When I arrived at the party, one of my favourite Latin American songs was playing, and within less than a minute, the migraine lifted completely and my body wanted to move to that music.

Music seems to affect the body at a very primitive level. It's as though the voice, limbs, head, muscles and even the breathing, all want to engage in the musical experience. In short, music makes us want to dance, and studies have confirmed that dancing really does make us feel happier. Because of this, I advise some clients who are feeling down to go home and put on their favourite piece of music, and to spend a bit of time just letting their body move to the music in whatever way it wants to, and to do this with nobody else around in order to be free of any inhibitions. For me, spontaneously moving my body to music is like embracing the energy of the universe, creating a real sense of love for life.

Singing

Having Irish, Welsh and English blood running through my veins, how could I not love to sing? To my mind, singing is one of the most emotionally-laden and enriching of activities, whether singing alone or with others. I know this because throughout my childhood, each morning at school everybody assembled in the main hall to sing hymns, welcoming in and giving thanks for the new day, and at 4pm the school day concluded with us all singing 'Now the Day is Over'. I have very fond memories of that musical routine and feel richly blessed in attending such a school. Singing those hymns with their rich powerful language and swooping passionate melodies, standing alongside hundreds of others as we sang in unison, all contributed to wonderful childhood experiences. I sometimes feel a bit sad that children attending our modern secular schools miss out on the stirring, heart-lifting experience of singing hymns as part of daily assembly with their fellow human beings. Whether or not you have a religious faith, singing hymns (or any stirring songs for that matter) can be an emotionally enriching experience.

There's a wonderful documentary film called *Cool and Crazy* about a Norwegian male choir. The visual and aural impact of these men (some of them quite elderly), standing in the wintry open air, singing their hearts out against the snowy alpine background of their homeland, provides a powerful emotional experience for the audience. The film captures the passion emanating from those men, manifested in their faces as well as their voices.

One of the things I would like to experience before I die is to attend a football match at Anfield in Liverpool (England) to watch the Liverpool football team play. I have to admit I'm not really a football fan, but being born and raised in Liverpool, I would like to experience being part of the group of supporters known as 'The Kop' as they sing en masse their special rendition of the song 'You'll Never Walk Alone'. I suspect this would be an emotionally enriching experience, but there is only one way to find out, and so this is now on my 'must do before I die' list!

Poetry/Prose

Reading our rich English language (especially aloud) can also be a moving experience. Even as a teenager, I loved reading the works of Shakespeare, reciting the powerful lines from his plays, words that would reverberate in my mind for the rest of that day and for the rest of my life. When I was fifteen, I was lucky enough to see *Macbeth* performed on stage and remember feeling charged with a strong emotion generated from hearing that powerful language. In the lines below, the first two are from *Hamlet* (Act 1, Scene 1) and the second two are from *Romeo and Juliet* (Act 3, Scene 5). Notice how Shakespeare uses the beauty of language to personify a new morning in these two different plays.

But, look, the morn, in russet mantle clad,
Walks o'er the dew of yon, high eastern hill.

Night's candles are burnt out, and jocund day
Stands tiptoe on the misty mountain tops.

Hundreds of years after Shakespeare's plays were written, his words can still provide an emotional effect through the beauty of the language. As well as being a talented wordsmith, Shakespeare's insight into human emotions makes him one of our earliest psychologists. Throughout his plays, many of the characters' emotional disturbances are manifested in physical symptoms, demonstrating Shakespeare's obvious understanding of how strong emotions can affect the human body.

When my children were young, I loved reading them the poem *The Pied Piper of Hamelin* by English poet Robert Browning. The stanzas have an almost sing-song, musical rhythm to them, and our favourite was the seventh which begins: 'Into the street the Piper stept' – describing how all the rats came running to the sound of the pipe. If you get a chance to read this poem, make sure you read it aloud to make the most of the richness of the English language. You will be in for a treat!

Art

I know there are many people who experience 'the sublime' in their appreciation of art. For me looking at paintings of people from other periods in history is a reminder that we also are just individuals living out our allotted bit of time on Earth, and one day we too will be long gone. Being mindful of the present moment, as well as the certainty of our own mortality, can enrich all our experiences with a sense of how precious life is, and quite apart from providing us with visual beauty and a piece of history, these paintings are immediate reminders of The Big Picture view of life. For me, this Big Picture view entails a continual awareness of being a living breathing human being on this planet, combined with the realisation that this is but a temporary state. Within the context of this larger perspective, even if somebody lives to be a hundred years old, a century's worth of time wouldn't even register as being a tiny speck on the cosmic scale of all that has gone before.

Many older paintings have a religious theme. One such painting that did move me emotionally was *The Pieta* by Gustave Moreau. This painting showed Mary lifting the body of her son Jesus after his death on the cross. The emotion I experienced was deep compassion more than anything else. I imagined what it might be like for a mother to witness her son being brutalised in such a terrible way. Crucifixion was common in those ancient times and I thought of the immense emotional sufferings of the mothers who might have looked up at their sons being slowly tortured to death on wooden crosses. I didn't attempt to imagine the physical pain of somebody experiencing crucifixion. I wouldn't allow my imagination to wander into such horrific excess. To me, the symbol of the cross represents a barbaric time in history, when atrocities of all gross descriptions were inflicted upon others. It makes me think – what a terrible time to have been alive! By comparison, our lives today are far more civilized, and this alone creates a strong sense of gratitude for being here now and not then.

Nature
Almost every morning when I wake up, I open the door of the bedroom and walk out onto the deck to welcome the new day. I'm fortunate enough to live in a beautiful place. My home is a small cottage situated on the edge of a harbour, surrounded by native New Zealand bush with hills in the distance. Whatever the weather may be, when I walk out onto the deck, I can see, hear and smell the beauty of nature all around me. Often at that early hour, the sea is calm, looking more like a lake framed by trees with the morning sunshine shimmering on the water. Sometimes there is a grey heron treading delicately along the shore, or a couple of tuis (native New Zealand birds) swooping gracefully through the trees. The chatter of birdlife in the background complements the scene.

It's on that deck at home that I often experience an emotion that could be likened to a gentle kind of blissful serenity. Each morning as I embrace the sights and sounds all around me, and inhale the fresh air, I feel grateful to exist, to be part of it all. I know that my life, and the life of every other living creature, is but a temporary thing, which makes our time 'being here' all the more precious.

If you truly love Nature, you will find beauty everywhere.
Vincent van Gogh

Although I'm not a religious person, the heartfelt emotion evoked by the beauty of nature stirs something within me, a feeling that could perhaps be described as 'spiritual'. It has the quality of some ephemeral fleeting memory. While I'm not sure what to believe in the spiritual sense, I do recognise that I'm experiencing a mystical type of emotion when encountering such beauty. This feeling can sometimes be so strong, it creates a sense of knowing (as opposed to wondering) that there is 'something else', but I don't know what that might be. Can being swayed by powerful emotions evoked by beauty be the same thing as a spiritual experience? The ways in which emotions can impact on our spiritual and philosophical beliefs are covered more fully near the end of the book in Chapter Eleven.

Animals

Being in contact with animals is high on my list of activities that provide positive emotional experiences. Whether it's a horse looking over a fence or a family of ducks on a pond, my heart gives a little leap of joy just to see them. The creatures that bring me most joy in life though, are the ones I have a close live-in relationship with – my canine and feline family.

The animal/human bond is very strong and having different species share your home and life with you can be emotionally rewarding. When I look at my cat, I see an exquisitely beautiful creature and the urge to reach out my hand and touch this wondrous life form is overpowering. I'm reminded of the saying – "God made the cat so that man may stroke the tiger." Although I'd love to stroke a tiger, Puddy, my domestic cat will do nicely for now! Having your pet cat or dog curled up next to you on the couch, hearing the cat's soft purring or the dog's contented sighs is joy indeed.

In return for our nurturing, the emotional dividends we gain from dogs and cats enhance our mental and physical well-being. Some hospital staff have noticed that dogs coming into the wards can have a positive effect on children undergoing chemotherapy. Doctors discovered that the children's adrenaline levels rose when being with dogs, which helped to bolster their resistance to the side-effects of chemotherapy. The company of dogs has also been observed to raise the mood levels of depressed patients. Not surprisingly, studies have shown that people who own pets tend to live longer and are generally healthier than those with no pets.

Animals and humans can have such a close bond that some people become depressed when their pets die. For many of us, our dogs and cats are close members of the family. They share our routines, they are non-judgemental and their love for us is unconditional, and when they die we feel the loss. Some people try to be helpful by suggesting that the owner should just go out and buy another dog or cat, overlooking the unique bond that had developed over the years between the owner and that particular animal. It's a bond that can often be stronger and even more special to a person than their relationship with human family members.

Children/Family/Friends

There's a great joy to be experienced being in the company of children, especially when they are little, when they are your own children and you love them dearly. To feel the warm small weight of your own baby close to your body usually produces loving and caring emotions. From an evolutionary standpoint, feeling like this obviously has good survival value as children being nurtured by adults is a necessity for our continued existence.

My children are now adults and the only way for me to recapture those years when they were little is in my dreams. When you are a busy working mother, the time goes so fast, and before you know it, the children have grown up and left home. When I see clients who are feeling stressed and frustrated with their young children, as well as giving them practical behavioural-focused advice, I sometimes say "Even though it might seem hard, savour having them in your life right now, because in twenty years' time you might remember how precious this period of your life really was, and give anything to have just one of these days back again."

As well as remaining aware of our own mortality, it can be valuable to keep in mind the mortality of all those who are important to us and who we love, because one day they are not going to be around anymore. Experiencing our interactions with loved ones while maintaining a full awareness of the transience of life can enhance the quality of how we relate to them, especially during difficult times. Although this may need some practice, it is possible to interact with others while at the same time having a continual awareness of their (as well as your own) mortality. This Big Picture view creates a shift in how we perceive our everyday life, which in turn helps to quickly dissolve emotions such as anger while enhancing feelings of love.

Like many of us, my husband snores loudly at times. When this happened, I used to become annoyed and nudge him out of his sleep to stop the noise. But now, when I hear the snoring, I think – that sound represents life, and one day I might be willing to give anything to have that precious sound back. Now I just cuddle up to his warm body and appreciate his being alive next to me, snoring and all!

It's not until somebody we love is taken away from us, or

when illness or an accident creates an abrupt change to our routine, that we realise just how precious our ordinary everyday life is. Often it's only in retrospect that we realise how happy and how lucky we were then. The lines below were written by American poet Mary Jean Irion and express the anguish felt when what we take for granted in our everyday life is no longer there.

Normal day, let me be aware of the treasure you are. Let me learn from you, love you, bless you before you depart. Let me not pass you by in quest of some rare and perfect tomorrow. Let me hold you while I may, for it may not always be so. One day I shall dig my nails into the earth, or bury my face in the pillow, or stretch myself taut or raise my hands to the sky and want, more than all the world, your return.

Austrian psychiatrist Viktor Frankl attributed his survival of several years in Nazi concentration camps to the power of love. He didn't know where his wife was or which camp she may have been sent to, but imagining her face and feeling the strong sense of love he still had for her, even in the grimmest of conditions, provided him with moments of bliss. The hope of seeing her again gave meaning to his suffering. The Nazis had taken every-thing from him, but they couldn't stop him thinking about his beloved wife. The love he had for her was a powerful emotion that enabled him to physically hold on to life when it would have been so easy to die. Tragically, Frankl's wife and most of his family did not survive the camps.

Follow Your Bliss

Now that I have provided you with a few of my own examples, could you name some things that can lead to powerful emotional experiences for you? If music is able to trigger strong positive feelings in you, then just within this category alone, there are thousands of musical pieces to listen to, making it easy to continue blissful encounters of the musical kind for the rest of your life!

Joseph Campbell, the twentieth-century mythologist's advice to us is to "follow your bliss!" But in order to follow something you need to know what it is. It's now up to you to gather ideas of how you could experience sublime moments, to seek out activities and situations that offer opportunities for deep joy and a sense of awe and wonder.

Contentment

What comes to mind when you think of the word contentment? In our modern times the idea of feeling contented seems to have developed negative connotations, as though it were synonymous with stagnation, complacency, a lack of initiative or simply settling for the mediocre.

Contentment is a feeling most marketing companies wouldn't want us to experience too often. Their job is to persuade us that what we have isn't good enough and that we need to buy something better. Imagine for a moment what it might be like if the majority of people living in our modern developed societies felt content with what they have, with no desire to acquire bigger, faster or newer anything. What comes to mind when you conjure up such an image?

Over the years I have seen quite a number of very wealthy clients, some of whom had not gained any sense of contentment from being rich. In fact, a common fear amongst these clients was ending up penniless and starving! Although it was a fear of poverty that drove them mercilessly towards financial success, neither their money nor their possessions ever seemed to be enough.

It's my belief that once our basic needs are met, the more things we accumulate, the worse we feel, and that a good recipe for contentment is a simple life. A house full of 'stuff' can be stressful in itself, not just because it makes storing and finding things more difficult, but because it means having too many choices. Whether it's choosing which pair of shoes to wear, or which recipe in which particular cookery book to try, too many choices can make us feel overwhelmed. I'm not suggesting we go without or not have things replaced or fixed if they break down, it's more about having just what we need or really want without superfluous possessions, the type of clutter that fills cupboards, drawers, wardrobes and every living space in our houses. It's hard to feel contentment living with an excess of unnecessary things, in fact, research indicates that once our basic needs are met, more money spent on more things does not lead to additional happiness.

If we were to live in a more contented society, not continually striving for possessions to make us feel fulfilled, then perhaps we would be less driven to work longer or harder, and may actually have more time to engage in real happiness producing pursuits. I know this type of hypothesising could be described as idealism on my part, and for many people there would be difficulties involved with trying to change to a simpler lifestyle. Nevertheless, I have seen many, many stressed and unhappy people over the years, enough to suspect that a societal change focused more on contentment than becoming wealthy would be healthier for us and probably better for our plundered planet too. Perhaps with the quickly diminishing resources on Earth, the time is approaching when we humans need to collectively embrace the gentle emotion of contentment rather than continually strive for happiness and fulfilment via the accumulation of possessions, monetary wealth and material status.

Over the last few years, I have made a real effort to practice what I preach and simplify my life. This quest began by disposing of the absurd amount of clothes I had accumulated over several decades. Somehow I had developed an emotional attachment to a lot of my clothes which prevented me from getting rid of them. They had become entangled with nostalgic memories – "Oh, I remember wearing that dress when…", so the idea of throwing out that particular dress became akin to erasing a special part of my past. I also harboured ideas of one day being able to get back into size 10 clothes – "If I could just lose a few more kilos." Or the hoarder's classic beliefs – "That'll come in handy some day" or "that's far too good to throw away!" By moving my thoughts away from the past and the future, and concentrating on where my life is now, I managed to complete a ruthless restructuring, so that only those clothes I currently wear have been allowed residency in my wardrobe.

From clothes I moved on to shoes, bags, jewellery, perfumes, bed linen, pillows and duvets (I had managed to accumulate six different duvets when I live in a fairly temperate climate!). From the bedroom I moved on to other rooms as the great purge continued. This involved stuffing ornaments, dishes, glasses, pots, cushions and even books into large plastic bags, which along with all the other unwanted belongings, were taken to the local hospice shop or put in a rubbish bin. The last room to be tackled (and the most cluttered of them all) was my home office. After a full day's work collating and sorting boxes of papers and books, areas of carpet not seen in years began to emerge.

My home now feels more spacious, its contents are simple and basic enough to disappoint any burglar! I know where everything is, and because of my limited wardrobe, it's much easier to choose what to wear each day. My clothes are now comfortable, the right size, and in colours and styles that suit me. After the purge, my reward was a strong sense of achievement and contentment. Contentment is a pleasant feeling. It's not ecstasy, but it does provide a certain peace of mind. Having a sense of freedom from clutter and taking charge of how I want to live is emotionally rewarding. Right now, I can honestly say I have no wish to buy any new clothes, shoes, perfume, jewellery or handbags. I may continue to glance in shop windows as I walk past, but I have no desire to buy. I am content and it feels good.

Gratitude

As with contentment, a sense of gratitude is a positive emotion, and of course these two feelings often go together. One of the saddest trends I have noticed over the last few years is the lack of contentment and gratitude people have for their bodies. We often take this wonderful machine that is the human body for granted – until something goes wrong.

Quite a few of the people I see in my working role are unhappy because of perceived physical imperfections. Influenced by the media, fashion and celebrity industry, these clients are often women. They blame their unhappiness on the shape of their legs, arms, breasts, stomachs, hips or bums. I sometimes ask such clients to close their eyes and imagine what it would be like if they had been involved in an accident and the parts of their bodies that they didn't like had been badly injured. After letting them spend a few minutes focusing their mind on such a situation and what that would be like for them, they then describe back to me what they see, what it feels like and how they are going to cope in that physically challenging state. When they open their eyes and are returned to reality, I ask them to touch the area of their body that they believe is a problem and see if they can feel grateful that it's healthy and functioning, to feel what it's like to be on their body's side, to love it rather than hate it.

For female clients who have been influenced by media-created images of what the female form should look like, I remind them that just over 100 years ago, being the height of fashion would have meant wearing a bustle at the back of their dress, giving the appearance of having a very large bottom, which was considered an attractive female shape. To me, fashion and appearance seem to revolve around somebody in the background working the angles, promoting ideas about what's 'in' and what's 'out', making large amounts of money from human emotion and gullibility as people's desires for admiration, acceptance and approval from others are exploited to the hilt. From my perspective, to live an authentic life means dressing according to your own preferences (not just mindlessly following a trend), to love and care for your body, and to be grateful for it, because without it you wouldn't exist.

To cultivate a sense of gratitude, it helps to be more aware of what you *do* have rather than focusing on what you *don't* have. This doesn't mean you can't have future goals, but to focus solely on what is lacking rather than what you already have is an easy way to create feelings of resentment, frustration, envy, restlessness, anger and powerlessness – all needless emotional suffering.

For me, reading history books is a good way of generating a healthy dose of gratitude, especially when reading about how people lived in previous centuries. I feel grateful that I'm alive today, and so far I can honestly say I have lived a truly wonderful life. I have, of course, had my share of sorrow, loss, rejection, fear, humiliation, loneliness, struggle and defeat, but unlike millions of people past and present, I have never experienced starvation, severe thirst, extreme pain (other than childbirth), and I have never had to try and survive during a war as my parents and grandparents did. I have never been beaten or raped, I have never had a serious illness or serious accident and I have never been destitute or imprisoned. I'm grateful for all of this. I'm grateful that I was born in the mid-twentieth century to good parents living in a democratic country, a country with free schooling and a free public healthcare system which helped me to give birth to healthy children. These are just some of the big important things in life to be grateful for, and of course, there are thousands of smaller things if you really start to count your blessings.

About a year ago, I saw a film called *Melancholia*. The story is about another planet entering our solar system and colliding with Earth. This beautifully crafted movie had such a strong emotional impact on me that I left the cinema feeling stunned.

It's an excellent film for reminding us of how privileged we are to be living on our beautiful and precious planet Earth, our home in this universe.

When *Melancholia* ended and the lights came on in the cinema, I was so thankful it was only a film. As the audience shuffled out in silence, each of us going back to our everyday lives, I felt a strong sense of gratitude to be still here, to be still part of this marvellous journey.

Chapter Three

The Power of Meditation

Truth is the offspring of silence and unbroken meditation.
Isaac Newton

Continuing with the theme of creating positive emotional experiences for ourselves via the activities we choose to engage in, I now want to introduce you to a widely used relaxation exercise called meditation. Regular practice of meditation provides a means of experiencing valuable emotions and has been scientifically proven to benefit both our physical and mental health.

The following pages explain the key principles of meditation and provide an illustrated step-by-step guide to meditating. Different modes of meditation are covered to help you find the one that best suits you.

What is Meditation?

Meditation is a method of disciplining the mind so that both mind and body can become deeply relaxed. And it's when we are deeply relaxed that the body's parasympathetic nervous system (which is involved in repair and rejuvenation) is switched on.

Anybody can learn to meditate. The meditation technique I teach is not physically demanding and provides a very relaxed state. Although there are a variety of techniques, the general principle of meditation remains the same. Let's now look at the steps involved for practicing meditation.

Breathing Meditation

The most basic meditation method is simply focusing your mind upon your own breathing. This involves sitting comfortably in the upright position (you can rest your back against the chair if you want to) and closing your eyes. Sitting upright means you won't fall asleep as easily as you would if you were horizontal. Once you are comfortable, simply focus your attention on observing how your own body breathes in and out without you making much effort on its behalf. Just become an observer, quietly noticing everything about your breathing. Some breaths might be long and deep, others short and shallow. Sometimes it might seem as though you have stopped breathing altogether, but if you wait, the breathing will automatically start up again. Notice the sensation of the air going in through your nostrils and out again. Just remain in the observer role, noticing how this wonderful machine that is your body, keeps you alive by breathing in and out.

This may all sound very simple, but if you have practiced the breathing meditation before, you will know that it's actually quite a difficult skill to master. This is because other thoughts can so easily take your attention away from focusing on your breathing. The human mind is accustomed to going wherever it likes, immediately attending to any thoughts that appear and making them the new focus. Concentrating all your attention on your breathing may seem very boring to an active and restless mind, but practicing meditation is a good way of gaining some form of mastery over it.

When teaching people to meditate, I start by demonstrating on the whiteboard what thoughts coming into the conscious mind might look like. If you look at the two diagrams opposite, the diagram on the left shows an empty mind with no thoughts. The other diagram shows how thoughts can just automatically 'pop' into the mind.

Disciplining your thoughts is the most difficult part of meditation which is usually why some people become frustrated and give up. Let's say you have been concentrating fully on observing your body breathing in and out for about ten seconds, but then you lose focus and realise a different thought has taken

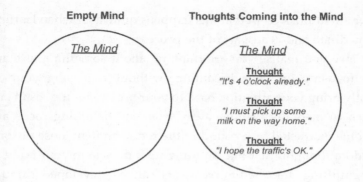

Empty Mind

The Mind

Thoughts Coming into the Mind

The Mind

Thought
"It's 4 o'clock already."

Thought
"I must pick up some milk on the way home."

Thought
"I hope the traffic's OK."

Example of the Breathing Meditation Process

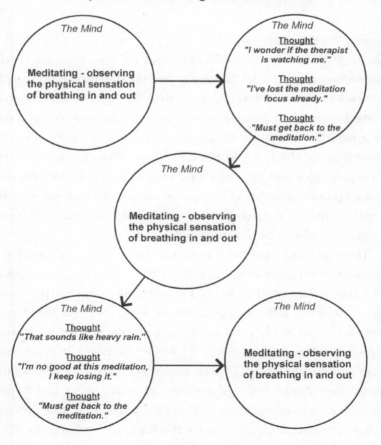

The Mind

Meditating - observing the physical sensation of breathing in and out

The Mind

Thought
"I wonder if the therapist is watching me."

Thought
"I've lost the meditation focus already."

Thought
"Must get back to the meditation."

The Mind

Meditating - observing the physical sensation of breathing in and out

The Mind

Thought
"That sounds like heavy rain."

Thought
"I'm no good at this meditation, I keep losing it."

Thought
"Must get back to the meditation."

The Mind

Meditating - observing the physical sensation of breathing in and out

your attention. Accept that this happens quite a lot when learning to meditate and is all part of the process.

Once you realise you are thinking about something else and not focusing on your breathing, without criticising yourself, gently bring your attention back to your breathing. It doesn't take much to mentally wander away from the breathing focus and become distracted by a sound in the room, an itchy nose or some random thought. Just like building up a muscle in your body by weightlifting, the meditative focus can be developed through regular practice. The diagrams show how practicing the breathing-focused meditation might look for somebody who is learning to meditate.

Mantra Meditation

The most basic form of meditation uses the breathing approach, but some people prefer to engage in 'mantra meditation'. This involves repeating a mantra rather than focusing on breathing. A mantra is simply a word or words repeated in your mind. It can be a simple word such as 'peace' or you can create your own mantra using any word or phrase. When choosing your mantra, it's helpful that you like the sound of it, as you may be repeating it to yourself thousands of times over. Also make sure you choose a mantra that doesn't conjure up something too specific in your mind, 'fish and chips' for example!

There are some people who insist that you should never tell anybody what your mantra is, but I can't see any good reason why this would need to be so. I created my mantra many years ago. I liked the soft easy sound of the word *soma*. At that time I believed I had made up a unique word, but years later I came across it in Aldous Huxley's novel *Brave New World*. In this novel, *soma* is the comfort drug given to the people of London by the controlling World State government to make them feel happy while they are being exploited! A few years after that literary enlightenment, while discussing the topic of meditation with a

Greek scholar, I found out that *soma* actually means 'the body' in the Greek language. Regardless of these other associations, I have not changed my mantra.

When teaching clients to meditate, I usually engage in the meditation exercise along with them. If somebody prefers to use a mantra rather than focus on their breathing, that's fine, but I still use the breathing meditation myself and there's a good reason for this. Many years ago, whenever I had difficulty getting to sleep at night because of an active mind, I would engage in mantra meditation using my word *soma*. Now, within even a minute of repeating my mantra, I can drift off to sleep. Naturally I don't want to fall asleep while I'm with my clients, so while at work, I only practice the breathing meditation. This still creates a wonderful sense of relaxation without putting me to sleep as the mantra meditation does.

Visual Meditation

Even though most clients are happy to close their eyes and focus on their breathing or mantra for the meditation relaxation exercise, there are a few people who prefer not to close their eyes. They like to visually focus on something that is relaxing, for example, a flickering candle flame or tropical fish moving around in an aquarium. If you prefer to meditate without closing your eyes, that's fine, a sense of relaxation can still be gained this way and the principle remains the same. When thoughts take the mental focus away from the chosen object (the candle flame), just gently return your attention back to the flame and concentrate your mind on only looking at that.

The Benefits of Meditation

By practicing any of these meditation exercises mentioned so far, even for just five minutes twice a day, you will begin to reap the rewards. The deeply relaxed state induced by meditation is beneficial for our physical and mental well-being. Studies have shown that people who are long-term meditators have stronger immune systems and are more resistant to disorders such as rheumatoid arthritis and even cancer, than those who don't engage in any deep relaxation exercises.

Practicing regular meditation has also been shown to significantly reduce the incidence of heart attacks and strokes, hormone levels are better regulated, and blood pressure and cholesterol levels are reduced. There is also evidence that engaging in daily meditation can be helpful with fertility problems, memory and digestion. In short, meditation is very good for our health.

Did you know that the human brain is capable of being physically changed? This is known as brain plasticity. Results from studies investigating the link between brain plasticity and meditation have highlighted some interesting facts. In these studies, brain scanning machines detected structural differences in the brains of those who regularly meditate compared to those who don't. Additionally, research has shown that people who are regular meditators generally feel more relaxed and happier, with better concentration and decision making abilities than non-meditators.

Many of my clients have experienced a profound sense of peace and relaxation by just sitting quietly on the couch in my consulting room engaged in meditation. Some described experiencing a strong sense of connection with their spiritual selves, something they had never felt before in their lives. A few clients have even described having an 'out of body' type experience! One particular man recently told me that without opening his eyes, he felt as though he was looking down at his own body sitting on the couch in the consulting room and that he could see me sitting on my chair. All I can say is that in the twenty-five years I have been regularly practicing meditation, I have never experienced such a thing myself, although I have had a sensation of light-headedness that has felt something along those lines, and which I put down to 'drifting off' rather than 'taking off'!

The benefits of regularly practicing meditation are considerable. It's an exercise well worth scheduling into your daily routine, even though life might seem too busy for you to accommodate this. If you are a very production oriented person, then the idea of sitting still apparently doing nothing might seem like an incredible waste of time. One way of overcoming this is to view your daily meditation as an activity that is important for your well-being, just as you might view regular physical exercise. Viewing meditation as actually *doing something* as opposed to *doing nothing* can be helpful in this case.

Meditating could be described as being awake but with a minimal level of mental activity going on. It can create such a relaxed state, you could even fall asleep and this may or may not be a problem depending on where you are. Meditation gives active minds a mini-holiday despite the repeated interference of other thoughts and continual refocusing of the mind. With practice, more time will be focused on the meditating as you develop the ability to abandon any new thought the instant you realise it's there, and return to your meditation.

Once established as part of your daily routine, meditating will become your own special haven, a place you can return to each day for a few moments of peaceful bliss. You will have gained a skill that will stand you in good stead for the rest of your life, enabling you to face the turmoils of life with a sense of inner calm.

Chapter Four

Being 'Stuck' in Negative Emotional States

We all experience feeling down, stressed or anxious now and again, but some people can become 'stuck' in these negative emotional states, which is hardly conducive to making the most of life. Apart from suffering at an emotional level, physiology and behaviour are usually negatively affected too. In this chapter, we're going to look at three common negative emotional states (being stressed, anxious and depressed), the relationship between these emotions, and the ways in which the suffering they cause can be minimised or overcome.

Stress

Most of us know what it feels like to be stressed, and we can usually recognise the types of situations that trigger this feeling. Examples might involve waiting in traffic queues, dealing with unreasonable people, noise, heat, unrealistic deadlines, faulty products, incompetent government bureaucrats and so on. Stress is mostly situational. Take the person out of the stressful situation and they are likely to come right. This, of course, highlights the importance of taking regular breaks, especially if you are in a stressful job or situation. Having strategies that enable you to effectively manage stress is important because ongoing stress can negatively impact both mental and physical well-being.

At a physical level, stress and anxiety can sometimes feel much the same, although anxiety is based on a sense of fear rather than frustration. Tensing the body when we are stressed usually leads to pain in the neck and shoulders as well as headaches, all of which can be aggravated by sitting for long periods of time in the same position (for example, being hunched over a computer screen). Relaxation, physical exercise and changing negative thoughts are helpful ways to combat stress. As stress is mainly situational, good problem solving abilities and being assertive enough to speak up for yourself are useful ways to bring about positive change.

People's levels of tolerance for stressful situations obviously vary. I know some people who are so 'laid back', hardly anything stresses them out, while others become emotionally uptight at the least inconvenient incident. In a crisis or a one-off stressful situation, our bodies are well geared to cope and recover from symptoms of stress, but when the pressures of everyday life seem relentless and overwhelming, that's when stress can become chronic and turn into anxiety or depression.

Anxiety

Anxiety is the most common emotional disorder I treat in my work as a psychologist. I use cognitive behaviour therapy to treat a variety of anxiety-related problems such as panic, phobias, PTSD (post-traumatic stress disorder), OCD (obsessive compulsive disorder), GAD (generalised anxiety disorder) and health anxiety (hypochondriasis). We human beings were never meant to be in an anxious state on a long-term basis The main characteristic of an anxiety disorder is that the fear is usually irrational because the sense of threat is based on something that is not really a danger within the current environment.

Fight or Flight

As briefly mentioned in Chapter One, the human body has its own built-in survival mechanism commonly known as 'fight or flight'. This developed to help our ancestors to survive by fighting or running away from life-threatening situations. We know when we are feeling anxious because, like any strong emotion, it manifests in our bodies. Common physiological changes associated with anxiety (and with stress) can include a rise in temperature (feeling hot and sweaty), rapid heart rate, dry mouth, diarrhoea, shaking, tense muscles, a tight chest, shallow breathing, nausea, prickling of the skin and 'butterflies' in the stomach. Tension in the body can be responsible for headaches, migraines, chest pain and stomach upsets, while skin-related problems such as eczema may be exacerbated.

When people are anxious, their regular breathing patterns can become disturbed, for example, breathing in shallow short breaths or even holding the breath. If hyperventilation occurs, this is when a sense of panic can take over as the breathing becomes out of control, resulting in feelings of nausea and dizziness. Hyperventilating creates lower carbon dioxide levels in the blood which is why people in this state are often given a bag to put over their mouth to breathe in their own exhaled carbon dioxide.

These physiological changes occur when we are anxious because our bodies are preparing to fight a perceived danger or run away from it. Both these activities (fighting or running) require physical energy, and to survive a pending threat, the body needs to be operating at its maximum effectiveness. Blood needs to be pumped around the body to the big muscles as quickly as possible, which is why the heart suddenly beats faster.

You could say that anxiety is like a well-meaning friend who is on your side, looking out for your welfare. So next time you feel anxiety symptoms, try to view these physical sensations as being your body's way of trying to look after you. If you ignore them, they will eventually go away. Working *with* anxiety and viewing it as the part of you that's trying to help, is far better than viewing it as the enemy.

Panic

A panic attack usually occurs when physical anxiety symptoms are misinterpreted as being dangerous. Common anxiety symptoms such as a rapid heart beat, feeling hot and sweaty, a tight chest and shallow breathing can cause the person experiencing these sensations to feel as though they are physically out of control or that they must have some serious illness. Any of these symptoms may feel uncomfortable at the time they are happening, but if they are only anxiety-related, they are harmless. A workout in the gym would have the same physical effects but without being a cause for alarm. However, for people who suffer from panic disorder, experiencing these physical sensations can seem terrifying, especially if they are alone or when in a public place from which they can't quickly remove themselves. Examples may involve being at the hairdresser or dentist, riding on public transport, being in lifts or in crowded places, or sitting in the centre row at the cinema or theatre.

Those who suffer from panic attacks tend to avoid a variety of situations, and even when challenging themselves to overcome the feared situation they might engage in 'safety behaviours'. For example, somebody facing their fear of going to the cinema is likely to make sure they only sit near the end of a row so they can leave easily should any anxiety sensations occur. This is their safety behaviour. With panic disorder, experiencing anxiety symptoms is usually the real fear, not being in a fire in the cinema or the ceiling collapsing, it's more a dread of feeling physically and emotionally out of control, and the likelihood of creating a public scene if they can't get out quickly. Another example of a safety behaviour might involve having somebody (a friend or family member) always within earshot so that help is at hand should they have a panic attack.

Being wary of where you go and how you get there, or feeling overly dependent upon others, obviously makes life very limiting, and there are some people who won't even leave their homes for fear of experiencing the dreaded anxiety symptoms. It's as though the terror experienced during the first panic attack (when the feeling of being physically out of control convinces them that they are actually on the verge of passing out or dying) leaves an emotional imprint on the psyche, making it something they never want to chance going through again.

If this description of panic disorder fits your experiences, before making any self-diagnosis, it's important to make sure that any uncomfortable or unusual physical symptoms are investigated by your medical doctor as they may be caused by some other physical problem. When the symptoms are caused by anxiety though, it's good to know that most people can learn how to overcome this debilitating yet fairly common problem.

The cognitive therapy treatment I use to help people overcome panic disorder involves teaching them to change the way they perceive their anxiety symptoms, so that they experience these sensations as being 'annoying but harmless'. Viewing them in this way removes any sense of threat. Along with the cognitive work, changing avoidance behaviour through gradual exposure to the feared situations is important. It's also important that the new way of thinking about anxiety symptoms is practiced while actually experiencing these sensations. Relaxation exercises (especially meditation) are useful for treating anxiety problems as they have a calming effect on the body's nervous system, along with learning to breathe in a more controlled way (the Abdominal Breathing technique is covered in Chapter Twelve).

Specific Phobias
Phobias are fears that usually develop after some emotional scare or they may be a learned behaviour, usually from a family member suffering from a similar phobia. Phobias are often irrational as the feared object or situation is not really dangerous. They can involve a fear of living creatures such as insects, frogs, birds, cats, mice or dogs, or inanimate objects such as needles or bridges, or even blood or vomit. These types of fears are called specific phobias. Certain situations such as driving or flying can also create great fear for some people (although in many of these

cases panic disorder is the real problem).

Phobias are maintained by avoidance of the feared object or situation. The short-term relief from anxiety gained by avoidance only aids in reinforcing avoidance behaviour as a long-term coping mechanism. Exposure to the feared object is often the best way of overcoming a phobia. Exposure can be graded (a bit at a time) or full-on (known as 'flooding'). In my experience, graded exposure is often the better treatment approach for phobias, although I did recently see a client (George) who wanted to overcome his fear of escalators by using the flooding technique. We met in a large shopping mall at 10am and spent the next few hours going up and down a variety of escalators. By 1pm, George was confidently using escalators by himself and was fully cured of his phobia – a very rewarding experience for both of us.

Jenny sought help for her phobia of dogs when she realised she was passing this fear on to her two young children. She felt as though she wasn't a good role model as a mother, especially as her two step-children (who lived in the same house), really wanted a pet dog. Not surprisingly, the conflicting emotions around dogs within this otherwise happy blended family were creating problems. Jenny's husband was reluctant to take sides, although he did like the idea of a family pet.

Therapy with Jenny involved graded exposure as well as relaxation training and education about dogs. We began with 'tiny steps' towards facing her fear. This involved Jenny agreeing to look at pictures of cute puppies, rating how anxious she felt and staying with this activity until the anxiety subsided. We then moved up a grade to pictures of adult dogs using the same process. After pictures, we progressed to real dogs. Luckily, I was able to borrow a cute Chihuahua puppy for Jenny to pat and hold in her lap. Holding the puppy continued until Jenny's anxiety subsided. The final stages of the graded exposure plan involved Jenny patting and being near adult dogs (my own placid and very well-behaved dog was brought in to represent the feared object). As before, Jenny rated her feelings of anxiety, staying with the situation until she felt okay. Her homework tasks involved visiting as many pet shops as she could in order to touch the puppies for sale, and her final assignment involved visiting the local SPCA (Society for Prevention of Cruelty to Animals) home for dogs and patting as many dogs and puppies as she could. By the end of the course of therapy, Jenny had achieved her goal which was to feel okay around dogs. Happily, the last I heard from Jenny was that she and her husband had adopted a puppy from the SPCA, and that the whole family had fallen in love with their new pet.

If you are a parent, it's good to avoid passing unhelpful phobias on to your children. By a parent's own fear and avoidance behaviour, he or she can inadvertently teach their children to be afraid of all manner of harmless creatures. I believe it's far better to teach children to have a healthy respect for other life forms combined with an understanding of how they function, rather than running away in fear each time one is encountered. In my own case, growing up with a mother who became hysterical if a bee came near, taught me to fear and avoid these creatures. As an adult, one of the things I did to help overcome this fear of bees was to find out all about them, which significantly changed my perception of them. Now I am able to calmly observe a bee near me without flinching or gasping as I used to, viewing them through new eyes, and with only feelings of admiration and respect. I realise that in certain situations and for a minority of people, a sting may warrant a real threat, but for most of the time these creatures only sting if they themselves or their hives are threatened.

'Healthy' Phobias
Sometimes having a phobia is not a problem. If you have a fear of sharks but you only like swimming in a pool, then this phobia

isn't likely to place any great limitations on your life. A common phobia is a fear of heights. The anxiety triggered by this fear can create a sense of being immobilised, as though we are 'frozen' on the spot and any attempt at moving seems terrifyingly dangerous. Like many people, I have experienced this feeling and it really is very unpleasant. A fear of heights could, however, be described as a healthy phobia because it obviously has some survival value. This particular phobia has been described as being an 'innate fear', meaning it's a fear we are born with rather than developed through experience. We may also be hard-wired to fear spiders and snakes, as avoiding these creatures in the past would have proved beneficial for the survival of our ancestors. I believe my mother would add bees to this list!

Social Phobia

One of the most common phobias is 'social phobia' which involves a strong fear of being negatively evaluated by others. This might include experiencing anxiety symptoms when interacting with others (especially in a social setting), meeting new people or public speaking. Blushing (feeling the face reddening and becoming hot) can occur when the social spotlight is on us. Whether the attention being received is negative or positive, for many people, to be singled out as the main focus of others' attention can seem like a threatening and uncomfortable situation.

It's well known that speaking in public is fervently avoided by many people. But why should this be the case when it's not a dangerous situation? Perhaps the answer is because it provides the potential to appear foolish or unacceptable in some way. I have thought a lot about this, and wonder if it could have something to do with the fact that we Homo sapiens developed as social beings, and standing out from others carried a risk of being rejected by the tribe, so keeping a low profile would seem safer. In our early ancestors' times, the loner would have been vulnerable as there really was 'safety in numbers', the tribe being the better social setting for survival. Therefore, putting yourself in the spotlight by speaking in public could be perceived as a situation for potential ridicule, disapproval or rejection by others. Engaging in public speaking is not a dangerous situation, but the 'perils' of making a faux pas or trying to cope with unwanted anxiety symptoms such as blushing, trembling, a dry mouth or your mind going blank creates the potential to be viewed by others as being 'nervous'. And when your body gives lie to the air of confidence you are trying to portray, there is the danger of being shown up in public as being a fake!

Because of anxiety symptoms and the risk of appearing foolish in front of others, public speaking is one of the most feared of all social activities. I remember many years ago when standing alone on the stage facing an audience, I could feel the saliva in my mouth drying up as soon as I began talking. This, of course made it difficult to speak audibly, and the embarrassment of how I might be sounding and looking (constantly licking my lips to help get the words out) created even more anxiety symptoms for me which only made things worse. From there on, whenever talking in public, I always insisted on having a glass of water nearby. There were still the visibly nervous signs of blushing and my hand shaking as I lifted the glass, but, as bad as these symptoms felt, to my mind, having a dry mouth when trying to speak was much worse!

Given my training in behavioural psychology, I knew that the more I exposed myself to the feared situation, the less anxiety symptoms would be triggered. And so I joined an organisation similar to Toastmasters called International Training in Communication (ITC) for women. As well as offering regular practice to speak in public, ITC provided opportunities to create speeches and present them at competitions all over the country. As I became more confident speaking in public, the shaking, the blushing and the dry mouth gradually disappeared, and I actually began to enjoy my time in the spotlight.

Although most people suffering from anxiety problems are not in a real crisis situation, the accompanying physical symptoms can make it easy for them to believe otherwise. As anxiety is associated with threat, the resulting behaviour is often avoidance. Those with a fear of social situations simply avoid putting themselves in the dreaded social environments, or they might turn to alcohol for 'Dutch courage' to help them face the 'ordeal' ahead. Alcohol tends to break down inhibitions, providing people suffering from social anxiety with some sense of confidence. Unfortunately, the consequence of drinking alcohol as a prerequisite to engaging in social situations can become an unhealthy habit with the potential to progress to more serious alcohol problems in the future.

Depression

O the mind, mind has mountains; cliffs of fall
Frightful, sheer, no-man-fathomed...
Gerard Manley Hopkins

We may sometimes hear people complaining about being "really depressed" when in fact they are just feeling a bit down or sad. Most of us feel down now and again, but it doesn't mean we are depressed. People can be mildly depressed, yet function reasonably well (although not enjoying life as much as they could be).

When people are seriously depressed, it's as though life is viewed through a dark lens. All seems negative. They see themselves as a failure ("I'm worthless"), the future is viewed as hopeless ("what's the point?") and the world seems overwhelming ("it's all too much"). Self-esteem is low and the behavioural response to all of this is often withdrawal. Physical fatigue and a lack of motivation make it difficult to get going, and a sense of enthusiasm (even for activities that used to be enjoyable) seems to disappear.

If you are suffering from depression, changes need to occur in two main areas. Firstly, you need to engage in looking after your body at a very practical level (self-care), which means trying to eat healthy food even if you don't feel like eating. It's the same with getting your body moving by doing some form of exercise, especially outside in the fresh air and sunlight. It might be the last thing you feel like doing, but physical exercise is helpful as it can trigger the production of endorphins in your body as well as increasing oxygen to the brain. Try to remain active, both physically and socially, as the urge to do nothing and withdraw from others can be very strong.

Secondly, you need to challenge negative unhelpful thoughts that make you feel miserable, reframing them to a more balanced and rational way of thinking (how to do this is fully covered in Chapters Five and Six). For those of you lucky enough to never have been depressed, it's important to realise that most people can't just snap out of it. Depression is a clinical disorder that affects the serotonin and dopamine levels in the brain. The best thing you can do to help is to be supportive. Sometimes depression does lift of its own accord, but generally people need to see their medical doctor which is when they might be referred to attend a course of brief therapy or be prescribed medication, or both. Treatment for depression often includes cognitive behaviour therapy which helps to change negative thinking and encourages behaviours that include activity scheduling, self-care, practical problem solving, mindfulness and assertiveness training – all helpful strategies used to combat depression and all of which are covered in this book.

The Relationship between Depression, Stress and Anxiety
Although depression can be triggered by a sense of loss without any anxiety or stress being involved, in my experience many

people who present for therapy with low mood and symptoms of depression also tend to have been experiencing high levels of stress or anxiety.

In the early days of my clinical training, my supervisor (a very knowledgeable and experienced behavioural psychologist) used to explain to me how problems with stress and anxiety can often lead to depression. He asked me to imagine a rat in a cage, the cage being wired so that the rat experiences intermittent mild electric shocks when it touches the bars on the left hand side of the cage. "Given this situation" he asked, "what would happen to that rat?" My answer was that the rat would become anxious and stressed, spending most of its time trying to avoid the shocks. This was a good answer.

My supervisor then asked me what would happen if the right hand side of the cage also became electrified so that the rat experienced intermittent mild electric shocks whenever it ventured either to the right or to the left of the cage. I wasn't sure how to answer this other than to say that the rat's level of stress would be very great indeed, to the point of becoming overwhelming. "Yes!" he replied, "and if that was the case, what would the rat do?" I tried to mentally put myself in the rat's place, but apart from feeling worn out with feeling stressed and anxious, I wasn't sure what I would do. There didn't seem to be anything the rat could do. My supervisor's answer to this question was that the rat would withdraw into a corner at the back of the cage and would give up trying to move. It would perceive itself to be in a hopeless situation and would eventually become depressed. From a biological perspective, in a situation such as this, the rat's stress levels would have been so consistently high that its adrenal glands would be depleted, making the rat vulnerable to depression. My supervisor described depression in this situation as being like a 'white knight' coming to the rescue of the angst-ridden creature and that winding down and withdrawing actually has some survival value as it conserves precious energy for the rat's possible future survival.

Over the years I have often thought about the analogy of the severely distressed rat becoming depressed and have observed the same process played out hundreds of times with people. When people are under extreme stress, their situation can begin to seem hopeless and they become depressed. This is a form of 'giving up' because they feel so exhausted and overwhelmed. When I work with such clients, once they begin to feel better physically and emotionally from the cognitive behaviour therapy, the emphasis of the treatment turns to teaching them some practical problem solving skills as well as assertiveness training. These skills involve action towards changing their situation rather than being like the rat in the cage and giving up.

Emotional Suffering in the Workplace

One of the most common areas where people suffer emotionally is in the workplace.

Being able to 'speak up' is usually a good first step towards solving work-related problems. Grant was a man in his early fifties who had worked for over twenty years in the same organisation. He enjoyed his job which involved helping people in a customer service role. Because Grant was so knowledgeable, friendly and approachable, other employees often came to him for advice, which made Grant feel valued and gave him a sense of confidence.

Unfortunately, the company was sold by the original owners and coming under new management, a process of restructuring began. With the threat of redundancy in the air, Grant reluctantly accepted the offer of a different position in the company. This newly formed role required a lot more technical knowledge and had a strong focus on sales (two areas where Grant felt out of his depth). The training he received for the new position was rushed as the trainer himself was overloaded and about to leave for a job in another company.

Very soon, Grant found himself struggling to cope with the new job. As the days passed, he became more and more stressed about his lack of ability to perform in the new role. His mind had been 'going blank' during the bits of intermittent training he did receive but rather than lose face and admit that he wasn't keeping up, Grant pretended otherwise. Several of his colleagues had been made redundant and those remaining were expected to work longer and harder, which they did for fear of losing their jobs too. Grant was reluctant to speak up about his poor training, as not only did he want to try and maintain his reputation as being the man who knows everything about the company, he didn't want to risk upsetting the new owners. Grant knew how hard it can be for people aged over fifty to find new employment, and especially with a CV showing over twenty years of service in the same company.

With the trainer gone, Grant was left to perform in a role he had little understanding of and even less desire to be doing. Each day he went to work, he sat at his desk and tried to look as though he knew what he was doing. Each day, his stress and anxiety levels rose as he worried about his future career prospects and the financial consequences of being unemployed. His hands were shaking, he was sweating and he developed a stammer. As well as this, his appetite, libido and sleeping patterns were all disturbed. Grant felt as though he was in a no-win situation, he couldn't do his work and he couldn't leave his job either. The day finally came when Grant felt that he couldn't get out of bed to face going to work. His doctor diagnosed depression as Grant had apparently ground to a halt both physically and mentally. At this stage he was referred to me by his doctor for cognitive behaviour therapy.

The therapy helped Grant to recover from his depression and provided him with some insight into how stress had been the originating problem. If Grant had stronger self-esteem and had been more assertive by speaking up as soon as he realised his training was inadequate, he may not have suffered the severe stress which lead to him becoming depressed. If Grant really didn't want to stay in that job, he needed a practical plan for the future. Unfortunately Grant's case is quite typical of the unnecessary suffering that people can put themselves through rather than risk the emotional discomfort and potential disapproval of speaking up for themselves.

Responding to Problems

Whether in a work situation or any other situation, we usually have options and choices as to how we respond to problems. We don't have to feel helpless and impotent like the rat in the cage. Even when we are in situations that are impossible to change, we can respond by choosing to be there as a temporary measure. With some escape plan in place (a future goal to work towards that will eventually change the current position), it's easier to view any difficult situation as being of a temporary nature only, and as such, better able to be tolerated.

> *Everything can be taken from a man but one thing, the last of human freedoms – to choose one's attitude in any given set of circumstances.*
> Viktor Frankl

Chapter Five

The Link between Thoughts and Emotions

...for there is nothing either good or bad but thinking makes it so.
William Shakespeare

So far we've looked at positive and negative emotions and how they can have a beneficial or harmful impact on our bodies and behaviour. But where do emotions come from in the first place? We don't just experience a strong emotion without something being the cause. The answer is how we think. When we experience emotions that feel good, we are usually thinking positive thoughts, and when we experience painful emotions, our thinking is likely to be more along negative lines.

As faulty thinking leads to inaccurate conclusions, so our emotional responses to situations can be based on a distorted view of reality. We can, however, train our minds to become aware of how we think, to be able to recognise and challenge faulty thinking, and to reframe irrational thoughts to a more reasonable and balanced view. In short, if we want to change how we feel emotionally, then we need to change how we think. Distressing emotions can be defused or even avoided altogether by simply changing the way we view a situation.

What are Thoughts?

Thousands of thoughts pass through our minds each day. It's important to realise that the thoughts occurring in your brain are not you. Thinking is a mental activity, so it's essential to separate your thoughts from the essence of who you are.

Many people suffer the effects of negative emotions when the thoughts causing them aren't even true. Such thoughts are based on assumptions that have been formed over the years by habitual styles of negative thinking. The thing that makes our thoughts so controlling, is that we tend to believe them, especially when they trigger strong emotions which in turn give credibility to the thoughts.

Most of us can learn to gain mastery over our thoughts by mentally 'stepping outside' of ourselves and becoming 'the observer', to see our thoughts for what they are – merely blips in the brain. Gaining mastery over our thoughts is a prerequisite to gaining mastery over negative emotions. Obviously, not all thoughts are irrational, but when strong negative emotions are being experienced, a careful and objective look at the specific thoughts that are fuelling these emotions often reveals some faulty thinking.

In my work as a psychologist, I often come across people who have been really 'taken in' by their own faulty thinking. Gina came to see me over how upset she was feeling because of her husband's family. She worked as an assistant in a women's fashion retail store and had married Mike, an IT specialist who came from a wealthy family of high achievers. Gina said she often felt intimidated at family gatherings because of Mike's family and particularly by her mother-in-law, who was the CEO of a large company. Gina loved Mike and believed that he loved her, but when interacting with his family she would maintain a low profile. She would not initiate conversations or offer opinions on anything for fear of saying the wrong thing and appearing stupid. As Gina became increasingly anxious around social events involving Mike's family, she created 'headaches' in order to avoid seeing them. She believed they looked down on her, that they viewed her as not being good enough for Mike.

When Gina and I explored the specific situations she presented as evidence of being put down by Mike's family, it became apparent that many of Gina's thoughts were actually faulty. In her interpretation of events and conversations, there was a strong bias towards the negative. It seemed as though Gina's 'psychological antennae' were finely tuned to detect 'slights' directed at her during family gatherings. It was Gina herself who seemed to believe she wasn't good enough for Mike's family. When Mike's mother tried to include her in conversations, Gina interpreted this as evidence that her mother-in-law was trying to set her up to appear foolish.

After completing a course of cognitive behaviour therapy, Gina's self-confidence was stronger. She became more open and natural with Mike's family and stopped comparing her occupational role to those of her in-laws. By being more open, she found out that Mike's grandmother had been a widow who had worked in a factory while raising three children on her own, and that this woman was held in high regard by Mike's family and viewed as an inspiration to their own successes in life. I reminded Gina of Eleanor Roosevelt's famous words – "No one can make you feel inferior without your consent." It's how we view ourselves that determines any feeling of inferiority, not the words or actions of others.

Although we can feel the strength of an emotion at a physical level, it's harder to recognise thoughts, especially those that flit across the mind as transient images. To provide an example, let's say you are a bit late returning to the city car park where you left your car, and it's now over the two-hour parking limit. In this situation, you might have a fleeting image in your mind of your car being towed away, and this in turn could impact on your emotions by making you feel anxious.

As well as being in the form of images, thoughts can play in your mind like a verbal commentary. Thoughts are able to jump from what's happening in the present moment to incidents that occurred in the past. Detailed images of past events and conversations can be played over and over in the mind. Thoughts may also be about what the future might be like, making assumptions and jumping to conclusions that often prove to be incorrect. Not surprisingly, our thoughts are sometimes irrational and unhelpful. Thoughts represent our internal dialogue – how we speak to ourselves – which can be quite different to how we speak to others.

Creating Our Versions of Reality

The Greek philosopher Epictetus (AD55–135) realised that it's how we think that creates our versions of reality rather than actual situations. He concluded that – "Man is disturbed not by things, but by the views he takes of them." As thoughts automatically pop into our heads, we tend to automatically believe them, paying little attention to whether they are true or not. This is despite the fact that thoughts can play havoc with our emotions.

Cognitive therapy is all about how we think. The founder of this therapy is American psychiatrist Dr Aaron T. Beck (who I had the pleasure of meeting at a CBT conference in England in 2004). Because cognitive behaviour therapy is so effective, it's now commonly taught to psychology students as part of their clinical training, and it was while completing the clinical papers in psychology at university some years ago that I first came across this very practical yet fascinating therapy. Studies have shown that cognitive behaviour therapy can be just as effective as pharmaceutical medication for helping people to feel better emotionally, and without any side effects. However, regardless of these findings, some people will need to be on medication in order to stabilise their mood and maintain well-being, whether they are in therapy or not.

At work, the model I draw on the whiteboard to help people to understand how cognitive behaviour therapy basically works is the Four Part Model. It's called this because it shows the link between thoughts, emotions, physiology and behaviour. How we think is linked to how we feel emotionally. How we feel emotionally is linked to our physiology which impacts on what we do (our behaviour). Each individual part of the model can make a link with any other part. The model below shows how these four areas link and inter-link with each other.

The Four Part Model

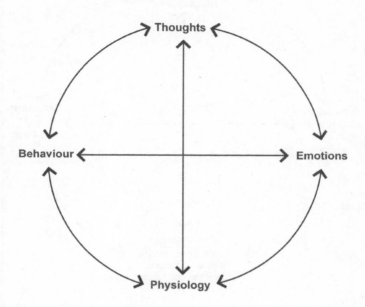

Let's look at depression on the Four Part Model. When people are depressed, thoughts tend to be negative. The negative thoughts lower the mood which creates an enervating effect on the physiology. Symptoms such as tearfulness, fatigue and lethargy as well as disturbances in sleep, appetite and libido are commonly experienced. When people feel like this, their behavioural response is usually to withdraw from others. Some people may turn to alcohol or drugs as a way of escaping from their miserable state, which of course can lead to even further problems.

The diagram overleaf shows how depression might look when placed on the Four Part Model.

The Four Part Model Showing Depression

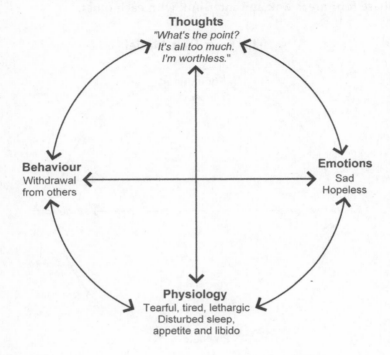

Thoughts
*"What's the point?
It's all too much.
I'm worthless."*

Behaviour
Withdrawal
from others

Emotions
Sad
Hopeless

Physiology
Tearful, tired, lethargic
Disturbed sleep,
appetite and libido

Looking at this diagram, the therapeutic work would need to focus mainly in the cognitive and behaviour areas. The negative thoughts would need to be challenged and changed to a more balanced perspective. Changes in the behaviour area would need to involve activity scheduling, self-care and problem solving. Somebody who is depressed needs to battle against feelings of fatigue and lethargy rather than give in to them. Going for a walk when you don't feel like it is better than lying on the couch staring at the ceiling and ruminating on how bad things are. By working in the cognitive (thoughts) area and the behaviour area, the benefits are felt in the emotional and physiology areas.

Let's look at how an example of anger (on the verge of turning into 'road rage') would look like on the Four Part Model. This situation entails Peter sitting in his car in a traffic queue. Just as the traffic begins to move, an inconsiderate driver pushes in front of Peter without indicating. The diagram below shows how Peter's angry thoughts can result in aggressive behaviour.

The Four Part Model Showing Anger

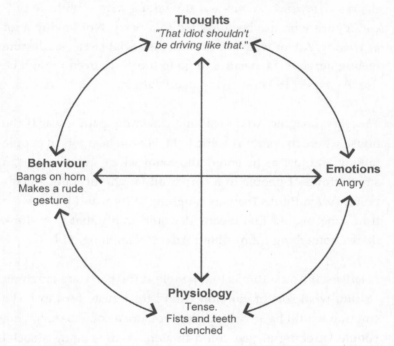

Thoughts
"That idiot shouldn't be driving like that."

Behaviour
Bangs on horn
Makes a rude
gesture

Emotions
Angry

Physiology
Tense.
Fists and teeth
clenched

If Peter could react to the inconsiderate driver by thinking something more along the lines of – "Well, he must certainly be in a hurry" – there would be less likelihood of anger becoming the emotional response, which in turn would not lead to physical tension or aggressive behaviour. When encountering these types of situations while driving, there is a little mental strategy I use which can be very helpful. If I feel myself becoming angry, I try to imagine that the inconsiderate driver is in such a hurry because he needs to reach his dying mother before she expires! It's amazing how my mood can instantly change from feeling annoyed to feeling sympathetic by simply deciding to change the way I view the situation. I find that feeling sorry for the driver is a much better feeling than being angry.

Let's now look at another situation people sometimes experience, and see how it would look on the Four Part Model.

Adam's Experience: Adam is a shy young man with little self-confidence who has been invited to a party. Not having a lot of friends, Adam wants to expand his social circle, so despite feeling nervous, he decides to go to the party even though he doesn't expect to know many people there.

Thoughts: Imagine Adam walking down the path towards the house where the party is being held. He can hear lots of people talking and just as he enters the room where everybody is, a small group of people in a corner all laugh out loud. At this point, Adam thinks they are laughing at him, and if this were true, what would that mean? It would imply that they think there's something funny about Adam, something odd.

Emotions: If Adam thinks that people at the party are laughing at him, what sort of emotion would this create for him? The emotion would be anxiety. Unless you are a comedian, having people laughing at you could be perceived as being a social threat. As a result of thinking like this, Adam feels anxious, self-conscious and awkward.

Physiology: Because anxiety is associated with a sense of threat, this would trigger some fight or flight physical symptoms in Adam's body. The threat here is that Adam believes he's being treated as an object of ridicule and the resulting anxiety symptoms cause his body to feel hot and sweaty (a blushing face and sweaty palms), his heart beats faster, he feels shaky and the saliva in his mouth is drying up.

These physical anxiety symptoms all contribute to making Adam feel very uncomfortable.

Behaviour: As in most anxiety provoking situations, Adam wants to avoid feeling like this, so he decides to leave the party and returns home. He tells himself "Never again! That's the last party I ever go to." Adam's thoughts have convinced him that he should never have gone to the party in the first place and reinforce his future avoidance of parties.

The next diagram shows how Adam's experience of the party looks when depicted on the Four Part Model. The specific event we are focusing on here is a group of people laughing at a party. Adam's interpretation (his thoughts) of this event created a very negative experience for him.

Adam's Experience of People Laughing at a Party

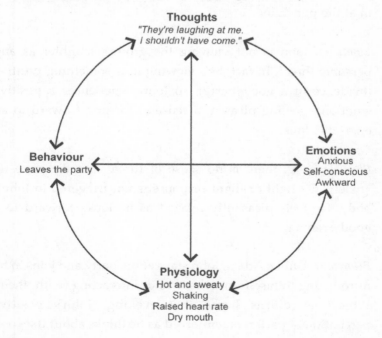

Thoughts
*"They're laughing at me.
I shouldn't have come."*

Behaviour
Leaves the party

Emotions
Anxious
Self-conscious
Awkward

Physiology
Hot and sweaty
Shaking
Raised heart rate
Dry mouth

Now let's look at another young man and his experience of the same situation at a party.

John's Experience: Unlike Adam, John is a confident outgoing young man. He has been invited to a party where he is unlikely to know many people, but nevertheless, he is still looking forward to going.

Thoughts: Walking down the path towards the house where the party is, John can hear the voices of people talking. As he enters the room where the party is being held, a group of people in a corner all burst out laughing just as he walks through the door. John's thought is "This sounds like a good party, lots of people enjoying themselves, laughing at jokes. Great!" Notice how John doesn't personalise the laughter as Adam did. John's interpretation of the laughter is that it's probably a joke or a funny story and he just happened to walk in at the punchline.

Emotions: John is not viewing the group's laughter as any personal threat. In fact, he's viewing it as something positive (evidence of a good party), so John experiences a positive emotion – feeling pleased, a sense of looking forward to an enjoyable time.

Physiology: As there is no sense of threat and therefore no anxiety, the fight or flight response is not triggered in John's body. He feels pleasantly relaxed as he looks forward to a good evening.

Behaviour: Unlike Adam, John stays at the party and joins in by introducing himself to others and interacting with them. When he returns home that evening, John's positive perception of parties is reinforced as he thinks about the good time he's had.

The next diagram shows John's experience on the Four Part Model.

John's Experience of People Laughing at a Party

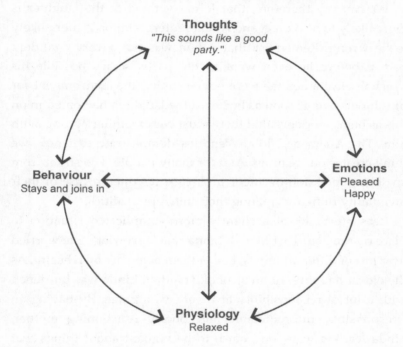

Both Adam and John encountered the same situation – people laughing at a party – but their experiences of attending the party were totally different. For Adam, it was a negative experience, but for John it was a positive experience. The difference was created by their thoughts. How the laughter was interpreted at the cognitive level created two very different realities. So which one do you think is correct? Adam or John?

You will probably answer that John's interpretation is the correct one, but why would that be the case? Why couldn't Adam be correct? The answer is that it's highly likely John's interpretation is the correct one because the very nature of parties often involves people standing about in groups talking and laughing. Imagine the organisation and choreography involved for a group of people to perform a collective roar of laughter just as one person walks through the door. It would be absurd, but that's not to say it wouldn't be possible. It's just highly unlikely.

We can say therefore, that John's version of the laughter is more likely to be correct and Adam's interpretation is more likely to be wrong. Remember that Adam was not a very confident person before he even went to the party, so it's possible his psychological antennae were out, scanning the environment for put-downs and as soon as he heard the laughter, he homed in on this as being evidence that there must be something 'wrong' with him. The Adam and John scenarios demonstrate that how we think creates our realities. And for many people who suffer from anxiety, depression or anger problems, it's often a case of their own faulty thinking creating their unhappy realities.

Let's now look at a slightly more complicated situation to place on the Four Part Model. Linda was 'a worrier'. She worried over lots of different things, one of them being her own health. As the eldest daughter of an alcoholic mother, Linda was burdened with a lot of responsibility at a very young age. By having an irresponsible, unpredictable and poorly functioning mother, Linda learned to be on guard, to be vigilant about things that could go wrong for her mother, as well as for herself and her younger siblings. Survival for Linda meant a need to be in control, to remain alert to any potential threat. Being vigilant and worrying became the mechanism she used to try and cope with life's unexpected events. Linda believed that if she didn't worry, then 'bad' things would happen. It was as though worrying was a productive activity that could somehow make a difference.

When her close friend died of cancer, Linda became convinced that there was something physically wrong with her own body, and that she too would soon be diagnosed with a serious illness.

This was regardless of recently having more than one thorough medical check-up. The symptoms that made Linda believe she was seriously ill were a rapid heart rate and a tight chest. These, of course, are symptoms of anxiety, but Linda (like many people with anxiety around their health) had been looking on the internet, and had self-diagnosed a range of life-threatening illnesses which further added to her already anxious state.

To see how Linda's situation might look on the Four Part Model, imagine Linda busy making a meal in her kitchen. Suddenly, out of the blue, her heart starts to beat fast.

Linda's interpretation of this persuades her that something is wrong. As her thoughts create a sense of threat, the resulting emotion is anxiety, which triggers her body into the fight or flight state. This in turn, makes Linda's heart beat even faster, causing her body to become uncomfortably tense. These symptoms now convince Linda that something is catastrophically wrong. Her behaviour involves constantly monitoring her body, focusing on her heart rate and noticing how tense she is feeling. Linda checks out her symptoms on the internet again in an attempt to explain her strange 'illness', hoping to gain some understanding of why her body is so 'out of control'.

The diagram representing Linda's situation is shown overleaf. Can you see that Linda's own thoughts and behaviour are fuelling her anxiety? They reinforce the idea that she's in a dangerous situation. This perceived sense of threat creates even more anxiety, and Linda's body responds by making her heart beat even faster (to increase the blood flow to her larger muscles so she can fight or flee). All this internal action occurs very rapidly and although Linda's body is really trying to help her to survive, she interprets this as further evidence of being ill and that her body is out of control. The 'danger' mode is fuelled by Linda's catastrophic thoughts and unhelpful behaviour, and is the type of vicious cycle that usually occurs during a panic attack.

Linda's Unhelpful View of Her Heart Rate

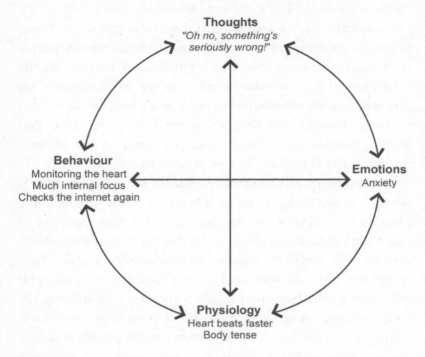

Thoughts
*"Oh no, something's
seriously wrong!"*

Behaviour
Monitoring the heart
Much internal focus
Checks the internet again

Emotions
Anxiety

Physiology
Heart beats faster
Body tense

Interestingly, a heart specialist told me a couple of years ago that about half of all patients rushed to hospital with a rapid heart rate or chest pain are suffering from anxiety rather than any specific heart condition. In Linda's case she was told by medical specialists that her heart was normal and healthy. When we exercise vigorously, it's actually good for our physiology to have the heart rate up, yet this same state can be perceived as being dangerous by those who suffer from anxiety problems.

Linda wanted to know why, when she was minding her own business making a meal for herself in the kitchen and not thinking any negative thoughts, should her heart suddenly start beating fast. Many clients ask this question and the answer is that sometimes physical symptoms do just come out of the blue. Often the person has been worrying about something, or is highly strung or stressed, and their nervous system just happens to fire up now and again, like a faulty alarm going off.

For Linda to help herself in this situation, she would need to change the way she thinks as well as changing her behaviour. Remember you only need to work in these two areas (thinking and behaviour) for the pay-offs to occur in the other two areas (emotions and physiology). The Four Part Model that follows shows how Linda could react to her heart beating faster in a more balanced and helpful way.

Linda's Helpful View of Her Heart Rate

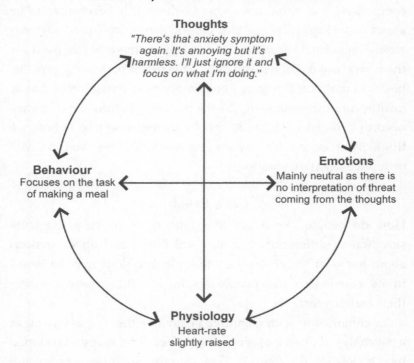

Thoughts
"There's that anxiety symptom again. It's annoying but it's harmless. I'll just ignore it and focus on what I'm doing."

Behaviour
Focuses on the task of making a meal

Emotions
Mainly neutral as there is no interpretation of threat coming from the thoughts

Physiology
Heart-rate slightly raised

It's quite possible to get on with whatever you are doing despite having a raised heart rate. It's not dangerous (unless you have a medical condition), and if you ignore it, it will eventually go away. But if you focus on your heart rate, monitor it or perceive it as something threatening, then the heart may beat even faster and be accompanied by a few other anxiety symptoms such as feeling hot and sweaty, nausea, tight chest, dry mouth or shallow breathing.

In Linda's case, she just needs to change how she thinks about her physical anxiety symptoms and change her behaviour to match the new thoughts. This is cognitive behaviour therapy in action. I'm pleased to say that Linda did eventually manage to overcome the worrying thoughts about her health, the consequence being a significant reduction in her anxiety levels.

How strongly we experience emotions has a genetic component, and some researchers believe this percentage to be about 50%. Regardless of any inherited predisposition towards strong emotional reactions, I don't believe there is any need for those who are passionate by nature to curb experiencing positive healthy emotions. Enjoying good emotions in a passionate way is healthy and life-enhancing. It's the negative, painful emotions we need to curb, and we can do this by paying attention to how we think. By changing the way we perceive situations, we can avoid or reduce negative emotions.

Core Beliefs

How do people like Adam and John come to view the same situation so differently and why did Linda end up so anxious about her own body? Answers to these questions may be found in the 'core beliefs' that people develop about themselves during their earlier years.

In conjunction with cognitive behaviour therapy, my work as a psychologist often includes schema-focused therapy (developed by Dr Jeffrey E. Young). This therapy involves uncovering people's core beliefs, which are the beliefs we develop about ourselves based on our experiences. These beliefs can be negative or positive, and may be triggered during certain situations occurring in our lives.

During childhood and adolescence, we develop ideas about who we are from our home life, our specific life experiences and from the wider world (school and friends). For example, if a child perceives that her parents' love and approval are conditional on her being a high achiever, then that child may develop a core belief about not being good enough as she is. From my observations, such people frequently do become high achievers as they can work really hard at trying to show the world that they really are 'good enough'. However, they can suffer emotionally when a situation doesn't work out well, for example, if they make a mistake or if they are overlooked for promotion. These types of events can activate their negative core beliefs because making mistakes or missing out on promotions would only confirm (for them) that the negative belief must be true – that they really aren't good enough.

Faulty thinking that becomes habitual often has roots in one or more negative core beliefs. If a person is lucky enough to go through adult life experiencing no difficulties, rejections or problems, then a negative core belief could lie dormant and not cause any upsets. Of course, this would be very rare as life isn't that easy. When difficult situations do occur, by recognising when our own negative core beliefs have been activated (often leading to irrational thoughts, negative feelings and unhelpful behaviour), we can learn to change this pattern by creating positive beliefs about ourselves. This makes us better equipped to enjoy life regardless of the usual trials and tribulations.

When negative core beliefs have been developed, there are likely to be some coping mechanisms to support them. Coping mechanisms involve assumptions about how we need to behave to keep us 'safe' from rejection or hurt. As an example, some people cope by maintaining a low profile because that's how they managed to avoid punishment, ridicule or disapproval when growing up as a child.

With some understanding of how our core beliefs and

automatic thinking styles create our realities and control how we feel emotionally, it's easy to see that the way we think is crucial to how much we enjoy our lives. The following chapter provides some useful strategies to help change negative thinking styles, which in turn minimises emotional suffering.

Most folk are as happy as they make up their minds to be.
Abraham Lincoln

Chapter Six

Minimising Negative Emotions

The sign of an intelligent people is their ability to
control emotions by application of reason.
Marya Mannes

If our aim is to enjoy life as much as we can by maximising positive emotions and minimising negative emotions, then we need to be able to recognise when our thinking is faulty and know how to change it. In this chapter I'm going to introduce you to twelve of the most common thinking errors, along with a variety of strategies and that will help you to recognise and change these irrational ways of thinking.

Faulty Thinking

Emotions are linked to how we think and if we abandon our ability to think in a reasonable way, then negative emotions are likely to run amok, making life frustrating and miserable. It may seem difficult at times to appreciate that we humans do have the ability to think in a reasonable and rational way because of our superior brains. Given the fact that we have highly developed brains compared to other living creatures, exercising our ability to reason in order to control unwanted emotions is important. As experiencing upsetting emotions involves suffering, gaining mastery over our thinking style makes perfect sense if we want to create a happier life for ourselves.

But how do we know when our thinking is faulty? A good indicator is how we feel at an emotional level. When we feel miserable, fearful or angry, these types of emotions serve as indicators to closely examine whatever we are thinking at that time. Just as we develop behavioural habits, for example, quickly putting lids back on jars or having a cup of coffee at 11am each day, it's the same with how we think. Reacting to events via faulty thinking habits is repeated over the years until it becomes automatic, making it hard to even know when we are thinking irrationally.

In Chapter Three the plasticity of the brain was mentioned and how regular meditation can actually change the brain's physical structure. It's the same with how we think. Studies have shown that how we think can impact on the architecture of the brain. Habitual styles of thinking create neural pathways in the brain, which is why irrational thoughts can occur so automatically they seem quite normal. When we learn to think in a different, more balanced way, this becomes the new cognitive norm. By thinking differently, new neural pathways are formed in the brain, making it easier for the more reasonable thinking style to be maintained.

So how do we begin to change the way we think? American psychologist Dr Albert Ellis was the founder of a therapy known as Rational Emotive Behaviour Therapy (REBT) which provides some useful ways to recognise when our thinking is faulty. In order to determine whether or not a thought is faulty, there are Three Main Questions you can ask. Firstly, is the thought true? Secondly, is it helpful? And thirdly, does the thought represent good advice, the sort of thing you would say to a loved one or somebody you cared for? Keep these three questions in mind as we look at some of the most common thinking errors (also known as thinking traps) and the ways in which we can be taken in by them.

Mind-Reading

A thinking error that creates much unhappiness is Mind-Reading. This occurs when you are convinced you know what others are thinking. Mind-Reading involves trying to evaluate how you are coming across through the eyes of others. The problem with this type of thinking is that it's based on guesswork because nobody really knows what is going on inside other people's heads. Whether you perceive people's thoughts about you to be good or bad, it remains conjecture, a waste of time and can be wrong. Drawing conclusions based on this sort of guesswork often leads to needless emotional suffering.

Examples of Mind-Reading could involve being convinced that somebody doesn't like you because they didn't return your hello, or that the boss is angry with you because you made a mistake (even though the boss hasn't given any indication that he or she is angry). Or you might believe that people are negatively evaluating you when you walk around town in your comfortable but rather scruffy track pants! People engaging in Mind-Reading usually have low self-esteem and are continually on the look out for signs of approval or disapproval from others. Scanning the social horizon for clues to help you determine if somebody likes you or not involves quite a bit of effort, which can make it a mentally exhausting activity.

If you suspect that you might be frequently engaging in this thinking error, how can you stop? Firstly, you need to become aware of how you are feeling emotionally as your emotions will be your cue. It may be that you are feeling anxious because you believe somebody is negatively judging you, (remember that anxiety is associated with a sense of threat). As an example, let's say you have just been introduced to your new boss and your thought is – "he doesn't like me" – which immediately makes you aware of feeling anxious (if your boss doesn't like you, then this could pose a threat to your career). You now need to find out if this thought is irrational by checking it against the Three Main Questions briefly mentioned earlier. The first of these being – is it true? You need to know whether the thought is a fact or whether it's just your mind jumping to conclusions. Could this thought, if it were verbalised, stand up in a court of law as being factual with evidence to support it? With Mind-Reading, the answer is usually no. Regardless of what our intuition might be telling us, the fact is we don't have the power to read other people's minds.

When you are in a situation where you feel convinced that somebody is negatively evaluating you, simply remind yourself – "I don't know what he's thinking because I'm not a mind reader." If somebody provides you with clear evidence that they don't like or approve of you (for example, you actually hear them say this), then this is factual, therefore it's not a thinking error.

The second question you can ask yourself is whether or not the thought is a helpful thought to believe. Does it subtract from your happiness? Engaging in thinking errors is rarely helpful as they usually have a damaging effect on self-esteem. It's far better to acknowledge – "this thought isn't helpful because it's making me feel anxious." Even if it is true that you heard your boss speak disapprovingly of you, it's not helpful for you to keep thinking about it because it makes you feel emotional in a negative way. If you can't *do* something about it, then just let it go.

The third question you can ask yourself is – "Is this how I would speak to a loved one or somebody I cared for?" For example, would you tell your friend that her new boss doesn't like her? The answer is probably no, because that could upset her. However, your thoughts represent your internal dialogue and this is how you are speaking to yourself. If you wouldn't speak to another person in the same way you speak to yourself because it would upset them, then why say such things to yourself? To help foster healthy self-esteem, speak to yourself with the same level of respect that you would have for somebody you care for.

Let's say you do have magical powers that allow you to look into other people's minds and see what they are thinking, and you actually see they don't like you, that they really do think you are stupid, mean or boring. Well, so what? Isn't it their right to think whatever they like? Remember that thoughts are just blips in the brain and everybody is entitled to think whatever they want to.

There are about seven billion people on this planet. Some people might dislike you simply because you remind them of somebody else, or they don't like your hair, or they are jealous of you. Well, so what? Although we might prefer to be liked by others, if you have strong self-esteem, you don't *need* everybody to like you. If your sense of who you are is based on what others think of you, then you have given away your *self*-esteem. With Mind-Reading, how you view yourself becomes conditional on what others might think of you. Therefore, in such a situation, you will spend a lot of time wondering what he or she or they are thinking of you, ruminating over whether that particular look or tone of voice was approving or disapproving. What an exhausting waste of time! If you are engaging in Mind-Reading a lot of the time, try to memorise the following three statements:

1. I don't know what others think because I'm not a mind reader.
2. Even if I could read minds and saw that some people didn't like or approve of me, well so what? It's their right to have any thoughts they like. Whatever they think doesn't take away my sense of value as a human being.
3. Most other people are probably more concerned about what *they* are doing rather than being focused on me.

When working with people who torture themselves by frequently falling into the Mind-Reading trap, I ask them to write the above three statements on a cue card and read them out aloud to themselves every day until the words become fully absorbed in their minds. Many have found this strategy to be very helpful.

For people who believe that others are admiring them or thinking well of them, I don't see any need for them to make changes. Even though they may believe something that's not true, it's not creating any negative emotions which would subtract from their enjoyment of life.

Fortune Telling

The thinking error known as Fortune Telling is all about jumping to conclusions. You know you are doing this when you are worrying about something that could happen, often attaching a negative spin to your prediction or making it a worst case scenario. There's nothing wrong with envisaging a worst case scenario and formulating a plan of action if it is likely to eventuate, but once you have done all you can, there's no point in continuing to ruminate on unknown outcomes.

Examples of Fortune Telling are thoughts such as – "I'll fail the exam" or "what if I don't get the job?" Rather than putting a negative spin on your prediction, you could think more positively – "I'll do well in the exam" or "what if I'm offered the job?" Of course both types of thinking, whether negative or positive, are jumping to conclusions, although it's the negative predictions that create the unpleasant emotions. A balanced way of thinking if you are about to sit an exam or attend a job interview would be – "I don't know how this will go, however, I have prepared as well as I can and intend to do my best at the time."

If you are worrying that something 'bad' might happen, then your thoughts are projecting a sense of threat. Unfortunately your body doesn't know the difference between conjecture and facts, therefore some fight or flight physical symptoms could be triggered. But as Fortune Telling is always conjecture, there's nothing to fight or run away from because nothing has happened. All the 'what if' drama is going on in your head, it's not happening in the real world at that moment. If you need to prepare or solve a problem around something that could go wrong, then act on whatever can be done, but after that there's no point in allowing irrational thoughts to ruminate in your mind. After all, this is just needless suffering because worrying doesn't make a scrap of difference to an outcome.

My life has been full of terrible misfortunes, most of which never happened.
Michel de Montaigne

If you are having difficulty letting go of a worrying thought involving something that could go wrong (even though you have some idea of how you would cope if the worst did happen), remember to apply the Three Main Questions – Is it true? Is it helpful? And does this thought make good advice to offer somebody that I care about? Remember that a prediction can never be a true statement of fact because in that moment of time it hasn't even happened. Once you have done all the preparation, contingency planning or problem solving that you can do, a more rational way to think is – "I don't know how this will turn out because I'm not a fortune teller, however, I intend to deal with anything that does go wrong to the best of my ability at that time" and then just get on with your life and stop worrying. For people who just can't stop worrying, even when challenging and reframing negative thoughts, make sure you read the chapter coming up on Mindfulness (Chapter Seven) as this will provide you with an extra backup strategy.

Catastrophising

How many times have you heard yourself or others 'making mountains out of molehills' when describing something that hasn't gone right? When we do this, whether thinking quietly to ourselves or verbalising the thoughts aloud, we are practicing the thinking error called Catastrophising. For instance, if you are describing something as being "terrible", "awful" or "shocking" when the situation is not of a catastrophic nature, then you are

Catastrophising. The language we use can have a strong influence on how we feel. When we use emotionally-laden language, we start to believe it really is *terrible* just because we left our bag of tomatoes on the shop counter, or that it really is *shocking* that the rates bill is going up again, or how *awful* that Ben didn't pass his exams. A more recent 'over the top' description now in common use is *gutted*. People describe feeling gutted over trivial setbacks such as their favourite football team losing, or when somebody doesn't get though to the finals in a TV cooking competition – "I was totally gutted!"

Listen carefully to how people talk and you will hear a lot of Catastrophising going on. Sometimes when I ring my elderly mother in Liverpool, she tells me with strong feeling how terrible the weather is because it's raining. She isn't talking about floods or storms, just gentle English rain! Using exaggerated language like this becomes a habit, and its frequent use tends to make us feel emotionally worse as we begin to believe it.

All thinking errors can become habitual, and being aware that you are thinking like this is the first step towards change. If you want to stop Catastrophising, as well as asking yourself the Three Main Questions, there is a useful little strategy called the International Scale of Awfulness (ISA for short) that works well. In my work, I often introduce people to the ISA by drawing a scale on the whiteboard. At one end is 0% and at the other end is 100%. Then I ask them to spend a few minutes thinking about something that they would describe as being 100% human suffering. This needs to be nothing to do with them at a personal level, but rather something that happened to one or more human beings anywhere in the world, and at any time in history. Maybe they remember something from a documentary film or a book. It needs to be something that actually happened, something that made them shudder and think – "Imagine what that poor person must have gone through!" Does anything come to mind for you that represents extreme human suffering, something you would rate as being 100% on the International Scale of Awfulness?

When a client has thought of a particular example, we place that at the 100% end of the scale. Examples of 100% human suffering commonly include the Holocaust, being trapped in one of the blazing Twin Towers in New York, being the victim of a tsunami or earthquake, or being in Rwanda when thousands of people were attacked with machetes and left to die. Some clients think of the awful cruelty inflicted on people in medieval times, such as being burnt to death at the stake. I remember reading a history book about how heretics (those who didn't believe in the teachings of certain religious doctrines) in 16th-century England were burnt to death at the stake. This was a particularly horrific death and in some cases it could take up to forty-five minutes of burning before they lost consciousness and died. Crucifixion took longer, maybe even days rather than hours.

Sometimes clients put forward situations that could not be viewed as being 100% suffering, especially when compared to the examples mentioned above. When somebody presents the situation of losing a house as representing 100% human suffering, I ask them "if losing a house is 100% human suffering, then what would losing a house and all your belongings, every member of your family, your community and your limbs rate?" In light of this being the terrible suffering that people in tsunamis and earthquakes have experienced, they reconsider their example.

It's interesting how people tend to only compare themselves with others from similar cultures and from their own period in history. This helps to explain why some people are emotionally unaffected when watching the TV news, seeing people from other countries suffering and dying in their thousands due to floods, yet be very upset at seeing flooding in their own country in which only a few people perished. This is why our Scale of Awfulness is international – we are comparing the sufferings of our fellow humans from all over the world – as well as from previous times in history.

The events of Sept 11th 2001 in New York left millions of people all over the world with a sense of shock and disgust. Whether to jump or to burn was a choice that many of those trapped in the burning buildings had to make, and hundreds jumped. Thousands of others on that day didn't have that choice.

Looking at the scale below, you will see that the Twin Towers catastrophe is at the 100% end. In view of this rating, where would you place your current 'catastrophe' in life?

The International Scale of Awfulness

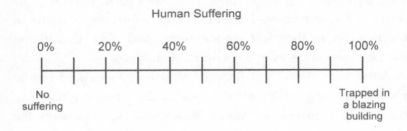

Human Suffering

To demonstrate how I make use of the ISA strategy in my everyday life, a few years ago, I was trying to drive home from Auckland city centre to Albany on the North Shore. I didn't get very far when all the traffic lights in the city went out (this was during peak traffic flow at 5pm) and there was not one traffic officer around to take control. The traffic on the road that led to the Harbour Bridge to get across to the North Shore was moving slowly, but the traffic on all the roads leading to that main road were in gridlock. I sat waiting in my car for almost two hours. It was as though anarchy had broken out, with nobody giving way and people honking horns, shouting and making rude gestures to each other. My hands were tense on the steering wheel and my knuckles were turning white with rage. My jaw was clenched and I heard myself say "This is terrible!"

At that moment, I was responding as though I were in a

catastrophic situation. To help get a more balanced perspective, I pondered upon what would rate as 100% human suffering on the International Scale of Awfulness. What came to my mind as I sat in my car was the Holocaust – an image of whole families of Jewish people being rounded up by the Nazis and herded like cattle onto a train bound for Auschwitz. And we all know that what happened to those people at Auschwitz really was terrible, shocking and awful.

Millions of people all over Europe in the Second World War endured atrocities and suffering we can barely imagine. On the ISA, being stuck in a traffic jam rates very low, not even 1%. Once I put a number on my situation (in all honesty this would be around 0.001% compared to the Auschwitz situation), my emotions moved right along the scale from right to left. Then I chose to use the more appropriate language to describe my situation. That traffic jam was frustrating and annoying, it was also somewhat disappointing to see my fellow humans behaving in such an aggressive way, but it wasn't terrible, awful or shocking as are real catastrophes such as the Holocaust.

Luckily, most of our everyday stressful situations don't even rate 1% on the ISA when compared to real catastrophes. Our difficulties may be stressful or annoying, but for much of the time they are 'small stuff' compared to situations that cause real suffering. So in a nutshell, the International Scale of Awfulness is a helpful strategy for putting our everyday stresses into a more balanced perspective.

Over-Generalising

When you find yourself having thoughts that include words such as *always, everybody, everything, never, all* or *nothing*, chances are you are practicing the thinking error called Over-Generalising. Most of the time, such thoughts are simply not true. Over-Generalising involves gross exaggeration. For example, if you burn the toast three times in the one week, you might think – "I always burn the toast", overlooking the fact that you didn't burn the toast on the other four days of the week. Or if three people at work tell you about the holidays they have booked, you think – "everybody's going away but me." This exaggerated way of describing events affects how we feel emotionally because we tend to believe our thoughts. An over-generalised style of thinking can make us feel frustrated, angry or even down, yet for much of the time, these thoughts aren't true. It's faulty thinking and as such, it can create unnecessary suffering.

If you want to think in a more balanced way, then the language you use to describe a situation needs to be appropriate to the situation. For example, if you hear yourself thinking in *always* and *never* type terms, ask yourself – is this really true? When you realise that it's not true, try changing to the more balanced view by using more appropriate words such as *sometimes* or *often*. Other examples of moderating language are – *some* people or *a lot of* people – rather than *everybody*.

Look at the examples below and notice how different you might feel at an emotional level when you compare the over-generalised statements with the more accurate and balanced versions of the situation.

Over-Generalisation	More Balanced Thinking
I **always** burn the toast	I **sometimes** burn the toast
	I **often** burn the toast
He's **never** on time	He's **often** late
	He's **sometimes** late
	He's **rarely** on time
Everybody's going on holiday	**Several** people are going on holiday

It's easy to understand how the use of balanced, reasonable language doesn't create the same negative feelings as thinking in over-generalising terms does.

Personalising

This thinking error occurs when you personalise situations that have absolutely nothing to do with you. For example, taking it personally and feeling responsible if others around you aren't happy, as though it must somehow be your problem. In our earlier example, we saw Adam falling into the Personalising thinking trap when he believed the laughter at a party directly concerned him.

Sometimes it's easy to even take the traffic light signals personally. For instance, imagine yourself in the following scenario: you are driving to a scheduled appointment and you are already running a bit late. As you approach the traffic lights, they turn to red and you have to stop. Then as soon as you are off again, the next traffic lights turn to red just as you approach. This happens again and again as you drive the length of the main road. It's as though the lights wait for your approach, then quickly change from green to amber to red when they see you coming! Taking this personally, you might ask yourself "Why is this happening to me?" or "What have I done to deserve this?" If you think in this way, then you are personalising a situation which is a random mechanical event. It has nothing to do with you personally at any level.

As well as traffic lights, taking weather conditions at a personal level can be a common form of faulty thinking. Hoping for a sunny day, Rosemary chose a date in the middle of summer for her wedding. The days leading up to this date were warm and sunny. She felt excited as everything was organised and ready for the big day. But when the special day arrived, the heavens opened and the rain poured down. Rosemary wondered – "Why me? Why today? What have I done to deserve this on my wedding day?" Of course, weather is completely indifferent to our plans. In such a situation, most of us would feel disappointed or annoyed, but there's no point in taking it personally, as this only leads to the "why me?" type of thinking which in turn leads to anger and a sense of being victimised.

Next time you find yourself personalising a random event, remind yourself that it's just one of those things that happen now and again and its occurrence has nothing to do with anybody at a personal level. If you become caught up in thinking "Why me?" try asking yourself the following questions instead – "Why not me?" and "What's so special about me that frustrating or disappointing events shouldn't be part of my life?"

All or Nothing

With All or Nothing thinking, there are only two ways of doing something, the right way or the wrong way. If something isn't perfect, then it must be a failure. Action is full on or non-existent. This thinking error is also known as Black and White thinking, and in my experience it tends to be perfectionists who think in this way. These people often work in jobs where making a mistake can have dire consequences, for example, pilots, surgeons or engineers. It's understandable that this dichotomous type of thinking develops because making a mistake in their line of work may result in the death of others. However, this perfectionistic trait can be extended into other areas of their lives, resulting in avoidance behaviour. Who would want to try something new when there is a strong likelihood of not doing it perfectly? They can beat themselves up emotionally if they make any mistake, even small mistakes that have nothing to do with their jobs. They may also use their All or Nothing style of thinking as a yardstick with which to judge others, sometimes becoming overly critical and difficult to live with.

We know that human beings are not perfect because we all make mistakes. All or Nothing thinking is very limiting as it only places people, their efforts and outcomes in the failure or success categories. As an example, Rob was complaining about a round of golf he had played at the weekend. He described his performance as being "absolute rubbish" and felt like a failure in front of his golfing friends. I don't know much about golf, but I do know they have a scoring system known as a handicap, so I asked Rob what his handicap was. He gave me a number, and then I asked him to look at a scale I had drawn on the whiteboard showing Failure/Useless at one end, Average in the middle and Perfect at the other end. Several grades representing Good, Very Good and Excellent were added, as were Poor, Very Poor and Dismal. I then asked Rob to place his golfing performance (taking his handicap into account) on that scale. He thought about this for a moment and decided that his performance in golfing terms had actually been quite good if he were to use the more balanced scale.

Rob is an example of somebody who was engaging in All or Nothing thinking by placing a good performance in the Failure/Useless category because it wasn't perfect. For Rob, the consequence of his own faulty thinking was unnecessary emotional suffering, which involved a sense of humiliation as well as anger towards himself for not being perfect.

Demands

If you often feel frustrated, guilty or angry, it's possible you are habitually engaging in the thinking error known as Demands. The language used in this type of thinking includes words such as *should*, *have to* and *must*. When this type of language becomes embedded in your thinking style, it can affect you in an emotionally negative way.

Thoughts such as "my partner *should* remember my birthday" or "I *have to* finish all the jobs on my list" or "I *must* mow the lawns every Wednesday" are irrational. They are demands about how things should be according to whoever is thinking in this way. Demand-type thinking makes it seem as though the thoughts themselves represent rules and regulations, God-given laws of the universe. But there are no such rules in the universe. The Demands thinking error can create rules about how the weather or how life itself should be, as well as how people should be. When things don't go the way we believe they should, this type of thinking makes us feel as though we have had our rights violated, leading to feelings of anger and frustration. Such demands belong in the Ideal World but we all live in the Real World, and in the Real World we only have preferences as to how we would like things to be. For example, "I would *prefer* to finish all the jobs on my list" rather than I *have to, should* or *must.*

There are other expressions we use which are really Demands in disguise. These are "if only" and "Why is it like this?" When we engage in *if only* thinking, we are not accepting something about the past. In other words, it shouldn't have been like that – "If only I'd done it differently!" The thought "Why is it like this?" usually involves not accepting something about the present because "it shouldn't be like this." In our earlier example, Rosemary was engaging in Demands as well as the Personalising thinking error in relation to how the weather should have been on her wedding day. Demand-type thinking literally insists that things should be or should have been a certain way in the present, future and the past.

If you want to take the imperative factor out of a 'should' statement, try changing it to a 'could' statement and feel the difference. The word *could* provides an element of choice whereas *should* doesn't, because it's a demand. Can you see how the language we use as part of our mental or verbal dialogue can create and fuel upsetting emotions?

Some years ago, I remember gazing in awe at the Grand Canyon. It was like looking at a snapshot of Earth's geological history, the layers of rock going back millions of years. It was at that moment I realised with great clarity that all our ideas about how things *should* be actually don't exist in this world. It's just idealistic thinking emanating from our own minds. That's not to say we just accept things as they are without striving for positive change in the world, but it's important to realise that language is powerful, and by simply changing the word 'should' to 'prefer' can create a slight cognitive shift which in turn creates an emotional shift, the result being less emotional distress. For example, thoughts such as "I would prefer that my husband remembers my birthday" or 'it would be nice if he remembers my birthday" are more balanced and less angst-ridden than the demand "he *should* remember my birthday!" After all, there are no rules in the universe to say that anybody should remember anything.

Pondering this statement, one of my clients concluded "Well, if it's a case of there being no rules in the universe to say I *should* anything, then I can just *prefer* to stay in bed rather than get up and go to work, right?" My response to this was to agree that yes, that's correct, there is no rule out there in the universe to say that anybody has to get up each morning and go to work, but there will be a price to pay for that choice to stay in bed, such as losing a job and having no income. So for people who don't want to do certain things but believe that the price for not doing them would be too high, it might be helpful to think more along these lines – "Although I might prefer not to do this right now, I'm choosing to do it." So in a nutshell, changing demand-type thinking by changing our language is a helpful strategy for minimising negative emotions.

Labelling

On making a mistake, have you ever called yourself "stupid" or an "idiot" or some other put-down name? When you do this, you are practicing the thinking error called Labelling. It's as though you are putting a label on yourself with the word IDIOT written on it simply because you made a mistake. If making a mistake constitutes being an idiot, then we are all idiots. Every person on Earth is a fallible human being. Nobody is perfect, therefore, labelling yourself with such a put down term doesn't make sense. And when a person calls themself an idiot or stupid enough times, he or she may start to believe it, which generates feelings of unworthiness. When an emotion is created by our style of thinking, the emotion makes the thoughts seem true, regardless of how irrational they are.

My clinical supervisor had a little saying in regard to the Labelling thinking error and it was this – "Proud to be an FHB" (FHB is an abbreviation for fallible human being). In other words, making mistakes is a normal part of being a human being. Mistakes mostly occur when our minds are preoccupied or when we aren't sure how to do something. By remembering that we are fallible human beings, we can view a mistake as a valuable learning lesson rather than beat ourselves up emotionally via negative self-labelling.

'Cantstanditis'

Some people have a very low level of tolerance for frustration, and as life is full of potentially frustrating situations from inclement weather to dealing with unreasonable people, it can be easy to fall into the 'Cantstanditis' thinking trap. This thinking error occurs when your thoughts are – "*I can't* stand this", or "*I can't* handle this" or "*I can't* cope with this." When you think like this, what sort of message are you sending to your brain? The message implies a sense of powerlessness – "I *can't*." As with any repetitious phrase, if you say it enough times to yourself, at some level you start to believe it. Next thing you know, mounting feelings of frustration and stress are making you angst-ridden and your body becomes tense and agitated. The truth is, for most of the time when things go wrong, you *can* stand it, you just don't like it. So once again, we are looking at how the language we use can affect how we feel emotionally.

Let's imagine a typically frustrating situation. You are standing in a checkout lane in a large supermarket. Your queue is not moving and the assistant at the checkout counter has her hand up waving for help from a supervisor as she continues trying to process a product with a faulty barcode. Minutes pass and you can see the queues on either side of you moving freely. Customers who had only recently joined the other lanes are walking out of the supermarket already served and here you are, still not served. So what do you do? You move from your 'unlucky' queue into one of the other faster moving queues. But then your new queue comes to a halt because of some similar problem at checkout and your original queue now begins to move quickly.

At this point you may start engaging in a range of thinking errors, such as "what have I done to deserve this?" (Personalisation), and tell yourself "it shouldn't be like this" (Demands). Or you might think how "awful" it all is (Catastrophising) or you say to yourself "I can't stand this!" Your body is tense, you are moving your weight from one foot to the other in an agitated manner, your jaw is becoming clenched and your hands are turning into fists. You look around in the hope of finding some external source of acknowledgement that what is occurring is totally unacceptable.

Saying "I can't stand this" to yourself is telling yourself a lie. If it were true, you would be in a collapsed heap on the floor. So if you are ever in such a situation and feel yourself becoming increasingly frustrated, check out what's going on in your mind. Try to change irrational thinking to something more balanced such as "I don't like this, but I *can* stand it." If you say this to yourself every time you become emotionally involved in a frustrating situation, you are likely to feel more in control and less distressed. It's also a good way of developing a higher level of tolerance for frustrating situations.

By accepting that frustrating situations such as slow supermarket queues are part of everyday life, you can cope without emotional stewing. If you choose to stay in a slow queue and simply wait, what could you do while waiting? Maybe you could look through the magazines that are often at hand, or you could observe what others have in their trolleys, or breathe deeply, or practice mindfulness (being aware of being in the moment of your life).

Emotional Reasoning

This thinking error occurs when you feel something so strongly at an emotional level that you believe it must be true. How many times have you been convinced that something is true based solely on how you felt about it? For example, on a day when everything seems to be going right and you are feeling 'lucky', you buy a lotto ticket, convinced that you are going to win – "I can just feel that this is my lucky day" – but you don't win. Regardless of how strong they may be, feelings are not facts. When we look at all the irrational thinking that can go on in our heads, and we know that how we think creates how we feel, it's not too difficult to conclude that the emotions we experience may sometimes be way out of touch with reality.

Some people ask me what the difference is between intuition and feelings. In my opinion, there's no difference, as intuition is a type of feeling. If you are picking up a strong sense of unease about something or somebody, this is often based on what you are identifying at a subconscious level. Minute signs that somebody's body language is incongruent with what they are saying or doing can be picked up at a subliminal level, providing a sense of something not being quite right. This is intuition at work. Some people really trust their intuition and act upon it without hesitation. However, to my mind, it's important to differentiate between what is intuition and what is the thinking error Emotional Reasoning, making sure that you are not simply interpreting feelings as being facts.

Disqualifying the Positive

How do you react when somebody makes a complimentary remark about an item of clothing you are wearing? Do you simply say thank you and feel quietly pleased that somebody admires your taste? Or do you perhaps feel awkward and try to debate the validity of the comment, saying something such as "What! This old thing?" which would probably make the person giving you the compliment feel a bit silly, the implication being that their judgement borders upon the ludicrous. Reacting to a compliment like this is a common example of the thinking error called Disqualifying the Positive. In other words, anything of a positive nature is not easily accepted.

When people have low self-esteem, any positive comments given to them by others can create feelings of awkwardness. Complimentary feedback doesn't quite fit with how they view themselves. Obviously, this type of thinking is faulty because it assumes that the person receiving the compliment is unworthy of any favourable recognition. It also discourages others from being open and natural in communicating their opinions.

When somebody gives you positive feedback about your work, how do you react? I remember a situation when one of my colleagues was being praised by her boss for the excellent way she had dealt with a difficult person. Instead of looking pleased and saying thank you, my colleague replied "I was only doing what I get paid for, what anybody would do." This is another common example of Disqualifying the Positive. Luckily, in this case the boss wasn't put off continuing to express his admiration for a good work performance. If you feel awkward accepting compliments or positive feedback, see what it feels like to just smile and say thank you, even if you don't believe you deserve the praise.

The Mental Filter

The Mental Filter is the last of the twelve thinking errors covered in this chapter. This type of faulty thinking occurs when we focus on the one thing that went wrong while ignoring all the things that went well, or ruminating on the one negative comment received while ignoring all the positive comments. As an example, imagine you have had a really good day, the weather has been lovely, and the radio was playing a lot of your favourite songs as you were driving home. You were still feeling good when you arrived at a social function in the evening, enjoying meeting up with your friends. Your whole day had been going well until you tripped up and spilt your glass of red wine all over the cream-coloured carpet while at the evening social function. Looking back on your day, you now think – "what a rotten day that was!" Because of the strong feelings of embarrassment at the social function, all the happy and positive moments of the day are filtered out, as though they never existed. This is the Mental Filter in action, resulting in an unbalanced recollection of your day based on one negative event.

In the above example, a better way of thinking would be – "It was embarrassing spilling that wine, but these things happen. On the whole though, I've had a pretty good day." Thinking like this, you may still feel some embarrassment, but you aren't likely to feel as miserable as you would be if you tell yourself how bad the whole day has been, physically cringing while you relive the spilt wine incident over and over in your mind.

Choose Your Reaction

Rather than allowing our thoughts to control us, we can learn how to control our thoughts. To change anything, whether it's your thinking or your behaviour, you first need awareness. You can't take control of a problem if you don't recognise what it is. By being aware of how you think (remember that your emotions will be the cue if something is upsetting you), you can start to check for any irrational thinking. You may find it helpful to write down your thoughts and see how they look. Analyse each thought by seeing if you can recognise any of the twelve thinking errors, or see how each thought stands up against our Three Main Questions:

1. Is the thought true? Make sure it is a fact rather than an assumption.
2. Is this a helpful thought? Even if the thought is true, why would you want to continue dwelling on it if it makes you feel miserable?
3. As thoughts represent our internal dialogue (the way we talk to ourselves), would you speak to somebody you love like this if they were in a similar situation?

If you come to the conclusion that the thought is irrational or unhelpful, then either change it to a more balanced way of thinking or try to let it go. If you are still struggling to change the thought, simply ask yourself – is there any other way of looking at this situation? Do you recall in the previous chapter how John perceived people laughing at a party to be about a joke or a funny story, whereas Adam perceived it to be about him? Remember that there are usually different ways of looking at situations, but when you are in the grip of a strong negative emotion, that's when you need to mentally step outside yourself, take a few deep breaths, and check to make sure you haven't been caught in a thinking error trap. Another helpful strategy you can use if you are struggling to reframe a negative thought is to think of a person whom you admire, somebody you would like to emulate, and then ask yourself the question – "How might he or she respond to this situation?" The answer might provide you with a better choice regarding how you want to react.

Optimistic Thinking
Thinking in a positive optimistic way not only helps to avoid or minimise emotional upsets, it keeps a spirit of hope alive, which

in turn encourages people to persevere and keep trying rather than give up. Optimists believe that things will eventually turn out okay, and as they are not easily discouraged by setbacks, optimists tend to eventually end up more successful than pessimists.

It is, however, very difficult to think positively all of the time, and some situations just don't lend themselves to being positive. But there is a way of attempting to turn a negative situation into a positive one by playing Pollyanna. Pollyanna is a fictional character who saw the positive in everything and everyone. So whatever was happening, she would find something good about it. For example, if Pollyanna were to be arrested and put in prison, she might think – "well, at least I'll have a bit of time to myself here." If she lost her purse she might think – "the person who finds it will make sure I soon get it back" or "the person who finds it will now be able to feed her hungry children, so by losing my purse, a mother's prayer for food has been answered." Few people would be able to keep such super-positive (and rather unrealistic) thinking going for long, but it's certainly a style of thinking that would help to minimise experiencing negative emotions.

Managing the way we think is an option we all have. In the terrible conditions of the Nazi concentration camps, Viktor Frankl was able to manage his thoughts so that he dwelt "in the spiritual domain, the one that the SS were unable to destroy." He endured unimaginable hardships and survived when many other prisoners perished. Most of our everyday stressful situations are really trivial compared to what Viktor Frankl went through, but we too can choose how we react to them. We can allow our thoughts to run wild, creating unnecessary emotional suffering and misery, or we can take charge and see thoughts for what they are – just cognitive blips in the brain that we can control and master rather than have them control and master us.

Balanced Thinking

There are some things we simply cannot do, and no amount of visualising or repeating affirmations towards an unrealistic goal is likely to make any difference. In fact, over-the-top positive thinking can often be unhelpful, leading people to feel disappointed and disillusioned. To provide an example, let's say I really wanted to win a sprinting race in the next Olympic Games. At my age and in my condition, regardless of what exercise regime I engaged in or how many affirmations I made, it would remain highly unlikely that I would stand any chance of beating the world's top athletes. If I were to cling to this unrealistic goal with all the positive thinking I could muster, I'm almost certainly doomed to disappointment.

Balanced realistic thinking isn't negative thinking. On the scale below you will see at one end the Extreme Negative View – "I can't do anything" – and at the other end is the Extreme Positive View – "I can do anything!"

Extreme Negative View	Balanced Realistic View	Extreme Positive View
I can't do anything	There are lots of things I can do and there are some things I can't do	I can do anything!

Both these extreme views are faulty because we can all do lots of things, but there are some things we just can't do – this is the balanced and realistic view. When people who are depressed come to see me saying they can't do anything, I ask them how they managed to get here, to get dressed and travel from A to B for therapy. Unfortunately, it's often unhelpful faulty thinking that contributes to their low mood. An extremely positive view may result in disappointment, but this is obviously better than the emotional consequences of taking an extremely negative and depressing view. The balanced view though, is the more rational and more helpful way to think, with less likelihood of emotional suffering.

Most of us have the ability to choose how we react to life's situations by managing how we think. Balanced thinking is important because it helps to create a healthy emotional state, and it's our emotions that largely determine how well we experience our lives.

We are what we think. All that we are arises with our thoughts.
With our thoughts, we make the world.
Buddha

Chapter Seven

Mindfulness for Emotional Well-Being

The ability to be in the present moment is a major component of mental wellness.
Abraham Maslow

In this chapter I want to introduce you to mindfulness and to the benefits that can be reaped by practicing this mental state of awareness. Mindfulness enables us to remain consciously aware of being in the moment as we go about our everyday activities, to be an observer of both our external and internal worlds, providing a sort of meta-awareness. We will also be looking at a type of mindfulness exercise known as *being* which involves stopping all activity to spend a few moments to simply acknowledge our individual presence in the universe.

What is Mindfulness?

In many ways, mindfulness is like a close cousin to meditation. By developing the habit of being mindful, you can generate a sense of calm and well-being as you go about your daily life. Rather than have your mind 'switched off' to the present moment while you ruminate on past or possible future events, practicing mindfulness allows you to become extremely observant, enabling you to fully concentrate on what's occurring in your current environment. Being mindful can also provide cognitive control as it allows you to select the type of thoughts you want as your main focus rather than putting up with unwanted 'mind movies'. In other words, mindfulness enables you to control your thoughts rather than have your thoughts control you.

Over the years, I've noticed that a lot of books and workshops seem to present slightly different mindfulness approaches, (although the principle remains much the same). To be mindful is to be mentally aware of what is happening in the moment, being where your body is and using your senses to help you take in the reality of your present environment. Most of my clients have found mindfulness to be very helpful, especially those people who can be plagued by unwanted negative thoughts which stop them from concentrating on what is currently happening in their external environment.

Examples of Mindfulness in Action

One approach to mindfulness involves being aware of three different 'states' of mind. Emotional State is when we are in the grip of a strong emotion (often because we are viewing a situation in an irrational way). Reasonable State is when we view the same situation in a rational and balanced way, and Mindful State is when we practice mindfulness. To provide examples which demonstrate this exercise, let's return to Linda who was mentioned in Chapter Five. This is the woman who was convinced that her rapid heart rate is symptomatic of some serious illness. Let's imagine that Linda just can't manage to reframe the thoughts that make her feel anxious – "It must be some serious illness" every time she notices that her heart is racing, and she just can't get away from this thought no matter how much she attempts cognitive reframing. At this stage of the therapy, the mindfulness technique would be introduced to Linda. As part of a therapeutic 'toolkit', mindfulness is an extremely valuable technique. The following diagram is of Linda's Emotional State of mind showing the negative thoughts that make her feel anxious.

Emotional State – Linda's Irrational Thoughts about Her Heart Rate

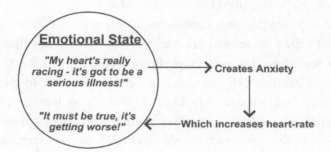

By reframing her unhelpful thoughts to the more reasonable view – "My racing heart is just an anxiety symptom that I've had before, it might be annoying but it's harmless" – this way of thinking becomes Linda's Reasonable State of mind. If Linda was to believe her reasonable thoughts, she may stay calm, accepting that the fast heart rate is harmless. This type of balanced thinking is unlikely to trigger further anxiety symptoms as it doesn't constitute a threat. The following diagram shows the more balanced thinking style of Linda's Reasonable State of mind.

Reasonable State – Linda's Rational Thoughts about Her Heart Rate

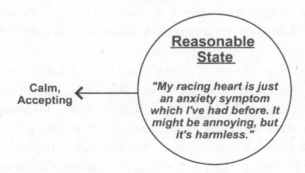

If Linda believes the thoughts in her Reasonable State of mind, then she wouldn't need to do the mindfulness exercise because she would be practicing cognitive therapy instead, which involves changing the irrational thinking of Emotional State to the more balanced thinking of Reasonable State.

But let's imagine that Linda's mind is like a television set. The channel called Emotional State is playing, and it's upsetting her. Linda switches channels from Emotional State to Reasonable State and decides "Ah yes, this is a much better way to view the situation" and tries to stay with it. But it's as though Linda's television set is faulty, and no matter how many times she switches to the Reasonable State channel, it keeps jumping back to the Emotional State channel.

In such a case, mindfulness is the next step. This involves mentally standing outside of yourself, being aware of your thoughts and realising that they are just blips in your brain. To re-emphasise an important point, just because we think certain thoughts and these thoughts make us feel emotional, it doesn't mean the thoughts are true. Continuing with the analogy of Linda's mind being like a television set, she needs to switch this off completely (losing both the Emotional and Reasonable State channels) and move into her Mindful State. The Mindful State represents a path that leads out of the headspace where the thoughts about her heart rate are occurring, and into reality, reality being her current external environment. The following diagram shows the three states of mind with Mindful State moving the mind's focus towards the external environment.

Mindfulness also helps you to be aware of what thoughts are 'playing' in your mind so that you can select to ignore any that are irrational or unhelpful rather than becoming involved with them. In other words – awareness provides choice. A useful analogy is to imagine standing on a platform in a railway station and noticing an express train passing through the station without stopping. Let any unwanted thoughts be like that express train and your mind the railway station. You notice the train, but you

Mindful State – Moving to External Reality

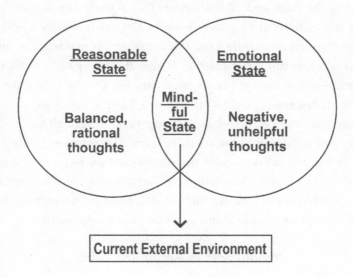

are not getting on board. Let the unwanted thought just pass on through as though it were an express train.

To employ mindfulness, the mind becomes focused on what is occurring in your current environment and what you are doing, so that you are really experiencing the moment we call 'now'. Use your senses – sight, hearing, touch, taste and smell – to help focus your mind on all that can be taken in from your external environment. Animals are very good at this, but we humans tend to allow our minds to wander off, maybe into the past ("if only..."), or worry about the future ("what if...?"). Meanwhile we are missing out on our present moment, the second by second now of life. The past has gone, the future hasn't yet come, the present moment is all we have.

Returning to our example of Linda, if she's cooking a meal, then that's her current reality and where her full focus needs to be – what she is seeing, hearing, tasting, smelling and touching. She might also notice anything going on internally, for example, being aware that her heart is still beating fast, but rather than staying focused on that, she chooses to return her focus towards cooking the meal and all the details that activity involves.

If the unhelpful negative thought ("what if this is a serious illness?") intrudes while Linda is focusing on making the meal, she could just think to herself – "There it goes again", as though the ruminating thought is an annoying fly. Or she could simply acknowledge the thought – "thank you, I appreciate you're trying to help me, but I'm okay", and bring herself back to what she's doing. Mindfulness helps us to be aware of when we slip back into unwanted thinking and promptly (and perhaps repeatedly) brings us back into reality, into the moment of life, the here and now of what we are doing. Below is a diagram illustrating how Linda can practice mindfulness while she makes dinner.

Mindfulness in Action for Linda

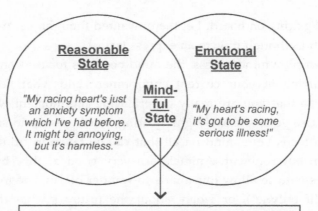

Reasonable State

"My racing heart's just an anxiety symptom which I've had before. It might be annoying, but it's harmless."

Mind-ful State

Emotional State

"My heart's racing, it's got to be some serious illness!"

Linda focuses on making the meal and all the details this would involve. Using her senses (sight, sound, touch, smell and taste) she observes what is happening in her current environment. If her focus returns to her thoughts in Emotional State, Linda chooses to bring her attention back to her external environment which involves making the meal.

To gain the most out of the mindfulness strategy, it's best to practice it when you don't need to, then when you do need to put it to use, it's likely to be easier. Some sport professionals use mindfulness as a technique to help them to focus being right in the moment of their performance. Any unwanted thoughts (whether they are true or not) can be controlled by using this strategy. If ruminating thoughts are making you feel miserable, why have them taking over your mind when you can be in the reality of your here and now environment instead?

For people who are weaning themselves off antidepressant medication, exercising mindfulness can be a particularly useful strategy. In this situation, some people excessively monitor their mood. For example, on waking up in the morning, the first thing James focused on was his internal state – "how am I feeling? I still feel tired, perhaps that means the depression is coming back." This type of monitoring tends to intensify physical sensations such as tiredness, and my advice to James and other people in a similar situation is to stop monitoring and just get on with everyday life. In the words of British author and philosopher Iris Murdock – "Happiness is a matter of one's most ordinary and everyday mode of consciousness being busy and lively and unconcerned with self."

A more helpful and balanced way for James to look at his situation is – "Just because I feel tired doesn't mean I'm depressed. Right now, I don't know if the depression will come back or not and my intention is to just get on with life. If the depression does return, then I'll deal with it to the best of my ability at that time." The following diagram shows how mindfulness would work for James.

If James were practicing mindfulness, he would try to stay in the Mindful State by concentrating on doing whatever he would normally do when waking up and getting ready for the day. This might involve showering, getting dressed, eating breakfast, reading the newspaper, watching the news and so on. All of these activities involve James using his senses to take in everything occurring in his current external environment (reality). If the unwanted thoughts of his Emotional State of mind intrude,

Mindfulness in Action for James

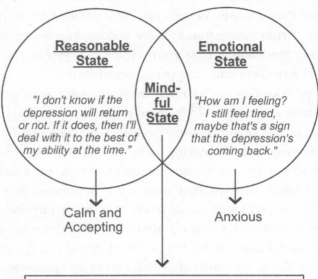

<u>**Reasonable State**</u>

"I don't know if the depression will return or not. If it does, then I'll deal with it to the best of my ability at the time."

<u>**Mind-ful State**</u>

<u>**Emotional State**</u>

"How am I feeling? I still feel tired, maybe that's a sign that the depression's coming back."

Calm and Accepting

Anxious

James' attention is on getting ready for work. He uses his senses (sight, sound, touch, smell and taste) to focus on what's happening in his current environment. If his thoughts return to Emotional State, James directs his focus back onto getting ready for work.

James could simply notice them, and think to himself, "There they go again, now back to what I'm doing", bringing his focus back to getting ready for work rather than allowing himself to become caught up with negative thoughts about the depression returning. Can you see how the mindfulness strategy puts James in control of what he wants to think and what he wants to do?

There's nothing to lose in letting go of unhelpful ruminating thoughts. They are of no value. If you need to *do* something in order to solve an existing problem, then do it. If nothing can be done, then let the thoughts go. Life really is too short to waste on negative 'mind movies'. Reality is where you are and what is occurring in that present moment of your current environment, and each of these moments is extremely precious because we only have a limited number of them in our lives.

> *The secret of health for both mind and body is not to mourn for the*
> *past, not to worry about the future, or not to anticipate troubles, but*
> *to live in the present moment wisely and earnestly.*
> Buddha

The Benefits of Mindfulness

Engaging in mindfulness by focusing on your current environment makes it easier to be spontaneous, to be authentically *you* without concern about how you might be coming across to others (Mind-Reading). You may enjoy a daydream about the past or even fantasise about the future at times. If the thoughts are not creating negative emotions or hindering what you are doing, then no harm is being done.

For couples who experience problems with enjoying sex, being mindful of the sensations of touch can be helpful. Focusing your attention on touching your partner's body during a massage, or focusing on the sensuality of being touched when your body is being massaged, provides an opportunity for the mind to stay in the moment, to concentrate only on the sensation of touch. Studies have shown that being touched can promote emotional and physical well-being and massage is a good place to start when trying to connect or reconnect physically with your partner. Sensuality eventually, and quite naturally, leads to sexuality.

Engaging in mindfulness is also a good way to generate some strong positive emotions. To provide a personal example, a twenty minute drive from where I live will take me to one of Auckland's magnificent West coast beaches, with its black sand and wild surf. To capture the full experience of walking along the beach, I use mindfulness to indulge all my senses in the moment-by-moment of the here and now. I feel the wind on my face, the warmth and texture of the sand on my bare feet. Breathing in deeply I can smell the salty sea air. As the big waves roll in and crash against the shore, I look beyond the waves at the horizon seeing nothing but a line of sea against the sky. This reminds me that I'm standing on a globe moving through space. I'm in my moment, both physically and mentally engaged in my environment. The result is a feeling of great joy to be here.

To illustrate the importance of being mindful, I want to tell you about one of my favourite British playwrights, a well-known and very talented man named Dennis Potter. His works include *Lipstick on Your Collar*, *Pennies from Heaven*, *Karaoke*, and *The Singing Detective*. Tragically, in 1994 Dennis was diagnosed with untreatable pancreatic cancer and given a very short time to live. Two months before he died, Dennis was interviewed on a British TV show by Melvyn Bragg. During the interview, Dennis only managed to keep going by taking liquid morphine and was very aware that it would probably be his last television appearance.

Some of the things that Dennis said during that last interview were truly inspirational. While working on his last play, trying to complete it before he became too weak to continue, Dennis described how he began to notice the blossom on a tree outside his window. Here is what he said:

> *...looking at it through the window when I'm writing, I see it is the whitest, frothiest, blossomest blossom that there ever could be, and I can see it... The only thing you know for sure is the present tense, and that nowness becomes so vivid that, in a perverse sort of way, I'm almost serene. I can celebrate life.*

Possibly without realising it, Dennis was practicing mindfulness – being in the moment of his life by really experiencing seeing the blossom on the tree. As his life's journey was about to end, everyday things such as the beauty of the blossom became very precious. He hadn't really noticed it before, probably because he was a playwright, a job that involved living in his imagination. I believe it's important that while we journey through life, we don't miss out on savouring each precious moment, and to stay fully conscious of the beauty around us. We don't need to be diagnosed with a terminal illness to appreciate how valuable each day is.

I remember early on in my career at a psychology conference I was required to present my research findings to a hall full of academics. Before giving my presentation, my negative internal voice was saying "what if somebody asks a question and I don't know the answer?" or "what if my mind goes blank in the middle of my talk and I come across as an idiot?" Needless to say, such thoughts guaranteed a feeling of anxiety as they involved the potential threat of appearing inept in the public arena. Cognitively reframing those thoughts looked like this – "if somebody does ask a question that I can't answer, then I'll simply tell them I don't know, and could offer to find out later for them." To reframe the worry about my mind going blank – "If my mind does go blank in the middle of my talk, then I'll just look at my notes and see if I can work out where I'm up to."

However, when I stepped onto that stage, I decided to practise mindfulness, to simply focus my mind on what I was doing, which was talking about my research. I resolved to really experience this event rather than dread it, and by staying in the moment of my life (second-by-second) up at that lectern, I actually enjoyed it. Certainly my heart was beating fast but that didn't stop me from functioning. Each day people are giving speeches, going to interviews or sitting exams despite anxiety symptoms. So next time you are required to engage in an activity that makes you feel anxious, try focusing on your environment and what you are actually doing. You might be surprised at just how well mindfulness works.

For me, an important part of mindfulness involves the continual awareness of my life's journey. This Big Picture view of life remains the important background when becoming immersed in the foreground (the present moment), regardless of how difficult the situation might seem. I think how lucky and how pleased I am just to be here at this time in history and in this place on the planet, to have been given an opportunity to have a go at life. So what if my mind does go blank in the middle of a talk or I don't know the answer to a question? To relish being alive, being authentically *me* in my 'bit of life' is surely the jackpot. And it's the same for you. Savour your time being alive on our beautiful planet Earth and use mindfulness to help you to do just that. As well as being mindful of your current environment, be mindful of The Big Picture perspective. Make the backdrop of each moment an awareness that says "Right now, this is it!"

The living moment is everything.
D.H. Lawrence

Staying in The Big Picture

So how can we remain conscious of the Big Picture concept of life? How do we live each day with the awareness that we are each a tiny piece of a huge galactic jigsaw puzzle?

A few years ago while travelling around the South Island of New Zealand, I came across a little place where early colonists from Scotland had attempted to settle in the new land. Unfortunately, that goal was not achieved. A lot died young, many others returned to Scotland. Most of the buildings were derelict, having been abandoned over a hundred years ago. There were however, some old black and white photographs of these early settlers on the wall of one of the few remaining buildings. One particular picture showed the children all lined up together in the front with the adults standing behind them, everybody dressed in their restrictive Victorian clothes. Looking at their faces brought tears to my eyes. The photograph created a snapshot of their 'now', capturing their time and place on Earth then.

I remember it being a cold and windy day as I wandered about the small graveyard situated not far from where I had been looking at the photographs. The names (along with dates of birth and death) of those lying beneath the gravestones were barely legible due to a covering of lichen. Sadly, most were children who had never made it to adulthood. I spent a few moments there, feeling the weight of the dashed dreams and loss for those families. It was a very poignant atmosphere, the only sound being the wind blowing through the long grass. Although sad, it was a good place to spend some time to simply reflect on the transience of life and how precious each day is. I felt grateful to be still alive, to be amongst the living above ground.

Being

The 'being' mindfulness exercise is all about just that – *being* rather than *doing*. This type of mindfulness involves acknowledging our own existence. Unlike meditation, *being* doesn't involve any focus on a mantra, breathing or a visual object. For people who find it difficult to experience joy from activities, by simply remaining still and reflecting on being alive in that moment, a different route to experiencing strong positive emotions may be discovered.

The Being Process

Engaging in the *being* exercise involves sitting comfortably in an upright position with your eyes closed, initially focusing on the feeling of your feet on the ground and your body against the chair. Then just notice in a gentle and non-judgemental way, any sensation or thought that attracts your attention. For example, sounds such as the ticking of a clock, the rain on the window or a rumbling stomach. Be like a non-judgemental observer, calm and quiet, observing any sensations or thoughts. Remember that thoughts are merely blips in the brain, coming and going all day long of their own accord.

When helping people to practice this form of mindfulness, I invite them to engage in an experiment as though they were a scientist by simply waiting to see what thought 'appears' in their mind of its own accord. This places the person in a state of simply *being*, they are not asleep, not thinking, not meditating, not doing anything, just waiting in a state of alertness, just like a scientist waiting to observe what blip arrives on the mind's radar. This can create a feeling of great calm and provides a sense of sitting comfortably in your own body doing absolutely nothing.

Sometimes when I find myself becoming caught up with the pressures of life, and my connection with The Big Picture perspective begins to slip, I spend a couple of moments to enjoy simply *being*. To help me make this a powerfully emotional experience, I mentally embrace The Big Picture concept – the miracle that here I am, a living, breathing organism on Earth, experiencing my short period of existence. I believe that by regularly practicing this gentle mindfulness exercise, a pathway to the authentic self is created, a pathway to the 'soul' if you want to call it that.

The Value of Contemplation

Sometimes it's hard to find a quiet time to simply acknowledge our own existence. In our modern world there seems to have developed an emphasis on experiencing life at a frantic pace, as though people are not allowed to simply *be*. Commercials on TV are full of rapid movement, images flashing wildly at us, the voice-over like a manic auctioneer full of mindless babble and urgency. With our brains bombarded by full-on action, it seems as though any opportunity for a quiet moment is viewed as time wasted, an unwanted vacuum needing to be filled with more noise and movement. Action-packed computer games and movies, often involving gratuitous violence, remain popular as 'entertainment' for the young. As human brains continue to develop until the age of twenty-five, regular exposure to such stimuli is surely of some concern for our society.

I recently read a book about the inventions and discoveries made throughout history, and observed that many of our inventors and scientific geniuses of the past had spent a lot of time during their earlier years just quietly thinking. In some ways I feel a bit sorry for children today, as well-meaning parents make sure that every hour of their child's waking day is filled. I wonder where, in all these action-packed childhoods, are the poets, the philosophers and the inventors of the future. I believe we all need some time to indulge our curiosity and our imagination, to have time for reflection, especially during the days of childhood and youth when the brain is developing.

I'm not advocating that you sit and 'navel gaze' for long periods, but spending some time (even for just two or three minutes each day) to simply *be* can provide a heightened sense of presence in your body and in the now of your life. As our lives are relatively short and fleeting, engaging in exercises such as meditation and mindfulness can provide a significant philosophical shift in how we experience our existence.

The nowness of everything is absolutely wondrous, and if people could see that... the glory of it, if you like, the comfort of it, the reassurance... if you see the present tense, boy do you see it! And boy can you celebrate it.
Dennis Potter (two months before his death).

Chapter Eight

Emotions and Healing

Although the world is full of suffering, it is also full of the overcoming of it.
Helen Keller

From both my work and personal life experiences, I know it's possible to harness the power of the mind via the emotions to help heal the body. This chapter looks at the mind-body connection and the strategies we can use that enable us to play an active role in healing ourselves.

Emotions have been found to play an important role in the healing process, with studies showing how positive emotions can have a significant impact on healing and recovery. Creating powerful positive emotions through the practice of mindfulness and deep relaxation exercises such as meditation, by how we think, and by engaging in happiness-laden activities, can all influence the quality and speed of the body's healing process. The opposite occurs when we are experiencing negative emotions. In short, our healing processes can be compromised or enhanced by our emotional state.

You only have to listen to how people express themselves – "I'm sick of this" or "he's a pain in the neck" or "she broke my heart" to realise we use everyday expressions that link our emotional state with our physical bodies. This makes some sense as emotion and physiology are closely connected.

Emotional Power and Healing

Many people believe that the physical body is merely a vehicle used to carry the all-important soul around the planet, and that when we die, we simply cast off 'this mortal coil', a bit like a snake shedding its old skin, while the soul lives on. In my opinion, you don't just have a body, you *are* your body. As our emotions, thoughts and actions are so inextricably linked with our physiology, it's difficult to see the body as simply being a vehicle for some separate part of us.

Love and Healing

One of the strongest positive emotions we can experience is love. Studies have shown that the euphoria people experience when they 'fall in love' with each other can have an incredibly powerful impact on their physiology. Passionate emotions were found to have the ability to block pain as effectively as powerful medications such as morphine.

When we love somebody who is suffering in physical pain, the empathy we feel towards them can be so strong, we actually feel their pain. Research into empathy and pain found that certain areas in the brain are activated when we feel physical pain, and these same parts of the brain are activated in people who simply witness somebody they love being in pain. This demonstrates the powerful connection between our emotions and our bodies.

As the emotion of love tends to be particularly powerful in the context of pain, injury and healing, I believe it's important that you love your body just as if it were your own precious child. If your body is injured or hurting, being caring, tender and compassionate towards yourself is important. Although we may not want to love ourselves in the same passionate way that a besotted couple might love each other, to my mind, having a deep love and respect for our own bodies is conducive to good health.

One word frees us of all the weight and pain of life: That word is love.
Sophocles

Conversely, studies have shown that a negative outlook can have a deleterious effect on the body's healing process. In my role as a psychologist, I often work with clients who have been physically injured, the injury resulting in ongoing pain that can last for decades. Over the years I have met a lot of people who don't actually like, let alone love their bodies. With their injured body no longer working the way it used to, some people develop such a strong loathing towards their pain and limited mobility, they don't want to even acknowledge the injured area as being part of their body, for example, a damaged arm or leg is viewed as the enemy. From my observations, hating your own body creates negative emotions that can impede healing, whereas feeling love and compassion, and a sense of tenderness towards the injured part of the body is far more helpful. Nurturing your body as though it is your own beloved child can provide an opportunity for the power of positive emotions to play a beneficial role in the healing process.

Venting Negative Emotions

Some people claim that having a good sob if they feel sad or distressed, or having a good scream if they feel angry, can 'clear the air' for them emotionally, providing a sense of healing that makes them feel better. They believe that letting it 'all hang out' emotionally is therapeutic and more conducive to good health than holding on to toxic negative emotions. Some research lends support to this idea, suggesting that venting emotions may have some benefits, but also advising that caution needs to be exercised as to when, where and how the venting takes place. Other studies suggest that expressing ourselves by sobbing, screaming or yelling is counter-productive because it maintains focus on the negative feelings.

From my own personal experience, I find that venting strong negative emotions is counter-productive. I actually feel worse after having a good cry. My eyes and face become red and swollen, I get a headache, and I feel ten times worse than I did before I allowed these emotions free reign. Of course, I'm not referring to those times when we are grieving or when really bad things happen, when it's hard not to cry. I'm referring to times when we feel stressed or angry, when things just aren't going right, or even when caught in 'hormonal storms'.

As with any strong negative emotions, an excessive feeling of anger is not good for our health. Anger now and again, and within the right context, is beneficial for society as it can provoke action for positive change. But expressing ourselves by shouting, swearing, accusing or using 'put-down' language every time we feel angry is not a good thing to do as it forms a destructive habit. To my mind, it's far better to either communicate how we feel in a constructive way at the time, or just let it go.

If you are somebody who believes that screaming, sobbing or yelling is a healthy therapeutic response to life's difficulties, you may not be doing yourself any favours. You could in fact, be alienating people who happen to be around during your venting episodes. When stresses build up, I find that connecting with my inner self via meditation, followed by happiness-laden activities is far better and much healthier than full-on emotional venting. I'm not suggesting we don't express ourselves if something needs to be said. Speaking up rather than accumulating negative emotions is healthy, but for most of the time, expressing ourselves can be done in a civilised and respectful way.

The Mind-Body Connection

Our bodies are superbly organised for self-healing. If you accidentally cut yourself, right away your body's healing process automatically swings into action. Your platelets clump, and blood in the cut area begins to clot. The body then creates a substance called fibrin which forms a matrix to start the skin's knitting together process. Should any infection occur, the leuco-cytes in your blood will gather at the site to fight the bacteria. All this mending and defending is going on without you having to do anything because bodies are naturally geared towards survival. However, how we think and how we feel at an emotional level can sometimes help or hinder the healing process.

How our thoughts impact on our bodies is demonstrated in the phenomenon known as the Placebo Effect. Many studies have shown that people who expect an improvement in their physical symptoms by taking a certain medication often experience an improvement, even though the medication may be nothing more than a sugar pill. If we really believe that something will help us, then we are likely to experience some benefits at a physical level. The Placebo Effect demonstrates how our thoughts and emotions are closely connected to our physiology. As well as positive expectations having a physical impact, researchers have also found that negative expectations can affect us too. When we expect to feel pain or nausea, we often do. As an example, I have observed people wincing as though in pain even though the needle hasn't yet touched their skin during a vaccination procedure.

To provide a personal example of the mind-body connection, I used to go sailing when I was younger, but I wasn't really a good sailor because I would feel seasick if the boat ever rolled much from side to side. Now, even when I'm standing on land looking out at the water and happen to see a boat rolling, I immediately feel the sensation of nausea. When this happens, I'm not on a boat, yet the recollection of how I felt (which is just a thought in my mind) is enough to affect my body.

Try this little exercise – imagine yourself picking up a lemon, taking a knife and slicing the lemon in half. Now see yourself picking up one half of the lemon, and squeezing it so that the pips and juice are squirting out. Now imagine picking up the other half and slowly pressing the flesh of the lemon against your tongue. Chances are that right now your mouth is salivating.

Although the lemon is only a thought in your mind, your body is responding as if it were real. People who have a phobia of spiders may only have to think about a spider and the hairs on their arms begin to stand on edge. Or sometimes the mere thought of an upcoming meeting with a particularly difficult person can cause an instant headache. These are all examples of the mind and body being closely connected. These types of experiences may be occurring all day long, some we might be aware of, but for much of the time we tend to not even notice as the mind-body connection is so automatic.

It's sobering to realise that the types of thoughts we have going on in our heads can actually make us sick. I know some people who won't listen to the radio news while driving home from work. This makes some sense because most news items tend to be about negative events such as rape, violence, murder, theft, riots and corruption, so why would we want such thoughts in our heads when they can create negative emotions that affect our bodies and influence our behaviour? For instance, making us feel too afraid to go out. Perhaps it would be better to spend our time listening to something uplifting such as a favourite piece of music while driving home, then by the end of the journey we might arrive home with a sense of happiness and well-being rather than sadness, fear, anger or disgust from what we heard on the news report.

Imagery

In an earlier chapter, we looked at how thoughts can actually create neural pathways in the brain. Many sport professionals understand this. Before physically competing, they conjure up in their imaginations a picture of themselves performing all the details involved in the upcoming tournament. I have tried doing this exercise myself. In my sailing days, it was often my task to pick up the mooring buoy with a boathook as we approached, and when I missed (which was easy to do) the yacht had to 'go around' so we could try again. But when I spent a bit of time seeing myself performing this manoeuvre in my mind before actually doing it, I noticed a huge improvement in my real physical effort. My arm was steady positioning the boathook as the buoy came closer, and my hand/eye co-ordination was exactly right for the pick-up. The reality of the physical manoeuvre was very similar to how it had been in my imagination. From then on, I became so good at picking up the buoy with the boathook that I hardly ever missed. So you can take it from me, using imagery before taking action can be useful.

As within the sporting realm, using the power of the imagination is now becoming more accepted and utilised as part of comprehensive treatment to help with healing. Clients I see who are suffering from pain as a result of injuries, and who want to make the most of their emotions and their mind-body connection to help with the healing process, often engage in healing imagery. This exercise involves creating three different sets of imagery as part of a strategy to help the body to heal itself. Let's now look at a few examples of how this works.

Paul had suffered chronic pain in his knee since a motorbike injury a few years ago. For the first part of the healing imagery exercise, I asked Paul to close his eyes and focus his mind on the area of his body where the pain was coming from. I then asked him to describe how he saw his pain. Some people can be very good at using imagery to describe their pain. In Paul's case he described the pain in his knee as being like a red hot volcano, spitting up molten lava.

Rachel created an image of her pain as being like a pit bull terrier clamped onto her elbow with its teeth. Another client (Aaron) described his back pain as being like red daggers moving in and out along his spine. These are all good examples of mental visualisation. When people find it hard to form a mental image of their pain, I ask them questions such as what colour is it? What shape is it? Does it remind them of anything? Is it hot or cold?

Sometimes I ask them to imagine they are a tiny scientist with a clipboard and pen and they have the ability to journey into their own body and approach the painful area, to take note of what it is like, the colour, shape, temperature, density and whether there is any movement or not. Unfortunately, there are some people who really don't have enough imagination to do mental visualisation, but with a bit of help most people can come up with something.

Once an image of the pain has been created, the next step is to create an image that represents healing. Paul's healing imagery involved seeing the red fire of the volcano in his knee changing colour from bright red to orange, and then from orange to pink, the volcano becoming smaller and smaller until all that can be seen is a small pink dot which gradually vanishes. Rachel's healing imagery involved cool sparkling silver-coloured liquid running down from her shoulder like a magic waterfall, filling the area in her elbow and seeing the pit bull letting go of its grip and gradually dropping off, leaving only the sparkling liquid. Aaron's healing visualisation involved a special energy in the form of a cool white swirling mist entering his body and enveloping the daggers in his back. When the mist cleared the daggers were no longer there.

Once we have created two sets of imagery (the pain and the healing), we then create a final image involving activities. This entails creating a mental picture of what that person would like to be doing if they were pain-free. Paul produced an image of himself playing football in his back garden with his ten-year-old son. Rachel had an image of herself playing tennis with a friend, performing powerful backhanders, completely pain-free. Aaron created an image of himself walking along a beach with his wife and his two dogs. In his imagination he could see himself walking upright instead of crouched over as he usually was.

In the activity imagery, all the details of the situation are noted. For example, the weather, what clothes people are wearing, and most importantly of all, people seeing their own bodies moving easily and comfortably, completely free of pain. To help make this exercise easier, I suggest they imagine they are the audience watching a movie of themselves being played on a TV screen, to notice how happy their faces look and how easily and comfortably their bodies are moving. By experiencing these activities repeatedly in their minds, neural pathways can be created, as though the person moving in their imagination is actually physically moving. Not surprisingly, these mental images usually have a strong emotional impact on the clients.

When ready to commence the visual imagery exercise, the person first relaxes by engaging in a short meditation. Meditation creates a very relaxed state so that the imagery to follow has fertile ground in which to take root in the mind. After several minutes of meditation we begin the imagery exercise starting with the pain imagery. This is quickly followed by the healing imagery and finally the activity imagery. The client simply follows what I'm saying, using their imagination to conjure up the detailed pictures as I speak. The aim is for the client to mentally immerse themselves in the imagery. At the end of the three exercises we talk about what worked well, what didn't work and if necessary, we fine-tune or change the imagery to enhance the experience for next time.

In all the years I have been doing the meditation/healing imagery exercises with people, there are very few who didn't find this a positive emotional experience. Although I mainly work with people who are in pain, this same technique can be used for people who are ill. The principle involves sending a message from the mind to the body in the form of images. The clients do this exercise when they are very relaxed and receptive to suggestion. The strong emotional experience combined with the meditation and imagery can provide a valuable means with which to aid the healing process. To maximise the benefits, the meditation and imagery work needs to be practiced on a daily basis.

Although meditation followed by mental imagery is a useful strategy for managing pain and to help with healing and recovery, I want to make it clear that for people who are in pain or who have been diagnosed with a serious illness, it's important to consider a comprehensive range of strategies to help with healing. These might include conventional treatments such as medication and surgery, as well as lifestyle changes such as having good quality sleep, eating healthy food and engaging in any physical exercise that may be helpful. The more natural approaches such as meditation, prayer, healing imagery, physical touch and laughter can also play their part. It's important not to underestimate the power of positive uplifting emotions such as a sense of awe, love or joy, or any emotion that pulls at the heartstrings. Utilising some or all of these strategies places you in a good position as you try to reclaim your healthy body. And while you are doing all you can, love your body and trust that it will be on your side, after all, your body is *you*.

'The Secret' and Healing

Using the imagination is a wonderful thing that most of us can do. The popular book called *The Secret* by Rhonda Byrne advocates that when we visualise and mentally focus on what we want, it will appear, according to the 'law of attraction'. I don't believe that just thinking about something (without any action on our part) would cause things to materialise. This seems overly simplistic. There is, however, some truth in the notion that if we focus mentally on something, it can create action on our part towards it, as in the well-known saying – 'Energy flows where attention goes'.

To use an example, if you really wanted a red BMW convertible and focused your mind on this regularly, I don't believe the car will turn up at your door with your name on it without some action on your part. But the fact that you would be focused on that particular car means you might be looking at what is available. You might spot just the car for sale with some special deal that you could afford, therefore your wishful thinking would have manifested in reality, but only via action on your part.

The same principle applies to healing. A strong focus on healing is likely to encourage some form of action. This may involve making regular use of some or all of the healing approaches available. If I were told by my doctor that I had developed a serious illness, I would consider using all the treatments and strategies available. At the top of my list would be meditation and healing imagery, and I would make sure I was engaging in activities that would provide me with strong positive emotions that are stirring and heartfelt. I would certainly be utilising whatever modern medical technology had to offer, being grateful for all the past and present research undertaken by medical scientists and doctors that now provides us with wonderfully effective options that were unavailable to our ancestors.

Fortunately, further research is being undertaken into the connection between our bodies and our emotions. I believe we have only scratched the surface of this important subject and any further studies may well provide some more surprising and valuable information.

In the depth of winter, I finally learned that within me there lay an invincible summer.
Albert Camus

Chapter Nine

Emotions and Communication

We have already covered how the language we use in our thinking style can have a powerful impact on our emotions, but what about the language we use when we verbally communicate with each other, especially when emotions are involved? Although we humans are blessed with vocal chords and can use language to communicate complex information to each other, including our thoughts, feelings and needs, we don't seem to do this as much as we could or as well as we could. This chapter looks at how to communicate with others in a constructive way in order to express how we are feeling emotionally and to get our needs met.

Communicating in a Constructive Way

Relying on non-verbal communication as the main way of gathering information can be inefficient and time-wasting when compared to using direct language. Yet, why do so many of us resort to this approach rather than use our vocal chords? The answer is that our emotions tend to get in the way of honest constructive communication. For example, do you ever become 'quiet' if you are feeling emotionally hurt, and convey how you feel by reducing your level of interaction? Some people might describe this as sulking, but to my mind, suddenly becoming unusually reticent is more about a sense of hurt which has affected the person's self-esteem in some way. It usually doesn't last long, but it's how many of us cope with hurt feelings. Real sulking can involve downright rudeness – somebody deliberately not responding to questions and ignoring the other, which may last for hours or days, or even longer. Sulking is obviously a destructive mode of behaviour in any form of a relationship, a type of emotional blackmail that is immature and unreasonable.

Alternatively, there are those who allow their emotions to become out of control when they feel hurt, ranting and raving like spoilt children. As with sulking, this behaviour is immature and unreasonable, and is usually evidence of poor people and communication skills. When we habitually allow our emotions to stop us from communicating well (by sulking or raving), the result is a lack of constructive communication skills, which in itself ensures that the vicious cycle involving unhelpful behaviour continues.

When a couple with relationship problems present for therapy, it's easy to quickly see that they are lacking good communication skills – a deficit that can allow their relationship to be sabotaged by negative emotions. Good communication in a relationship means being able to express yourself in an assertive way. Assertive doesn't mean aggressive, it's simply using language in the most constructive way. This can be done in a gentle and respectful way, or in a firm (but not aggressive) way.

If you look at the scale below, it shows passivity (not speaking up for yourself) at one end and aggression (using an angry tone and 'put-down' language) at the other. In the middle is the assertive style, which is communicating in a constructive and clear way.

Passive   Assertive   Aggressive

We are all on this scale somewhere and not always in the same place. We may be passive at work, yet assertive at home, or vice-versa. How you communicate your needs is important, and choosing to interact in an assertive style is usually the most effective way of getting your needs met.

Passive Mode

Having a passive approach means you are not saying what you

really want to say for fear of confrontation. Some examples might include not asking others to help around the house, allowing somebody to always have what they want, often at the expense of your needs, or not requesting that a person stops doing something that's upsetting you. Passive people usually seek approval or avoid disapproval, so they will often make a great effort to please others while putting their own wants and needs on hold. In work situations, they may volunteer to take on extra tasks that nobody else wants to do. Unfortunately, passive people can often be exploited and their good natures taken advantage of by others, including their own friends, colleagues, partners and family members.

So why are some people so passive? The answer is generally low self-esteem, although there can also be aspects of learned behaviour – "this is the way my father was." Perhaps they developed some negative core beliefs about themselves from their past experiences, making them feel as though they need other people to approve of them in order to feel good about themselves. The irony of this is that people who operate in a passive way usually end up feeling negative about themselves rather than anything else. Although we can all be passive now and again, if this is the usual way of interacting with others, then there's a risk of anger and resentment becoming 'bottled up', which may eventually result in an emotional outburst or turn into depression.

People who are overly passive can feel as though they are not living their own lives, that they are not on the playing field of life. Because they aren't speaking up about their needs, their needs aren't being met. They can be like the 'candle in the wind', blown about in all different directions by their effort to fit in with what others want. They allow others to choose for them, they don't 'rock the boat' or confront, and will try to pretend that everything's fine when it's not.

Passive people can become angry with themselves for not

speaking up, and angry with others for expecting them to be so flexible. The anger of the passive person tends to be covert, meaning that it's hidden anger. Sometimes they may not even recognise this themselves and it can take only one little thing more to go wrong for the pent-up anger to erupt, leaving that very nice person at the mercy of an emotional outburst. This of course, will cause great surprise to others as it would seem so out of character. Although a passive person comes across as being very nice, flexible and helpful, this approach to life is often not good for their own mental and physical well-being.

Being passive and being 'laid back' are two different things. Some people have a natural *laissez-faire* approach to life. They really don't mind being flexible and agreeable a lot of the time. The difference between this and passivity is that the passive person stews emotionally because they are agreeing to do something they don't really want to do, whereas the naturally laid-back person doesn't stew because they really are flexible, not minding one way or the other.

Aggressive Mode
An aggressive person often has an angry tone to their voice; their language may include 'put-down' remarks about other people, even to a person's face. They don't care much about how their aggressive manner might upset others and generally come across as bullying, cynical and hostile. There are those who might interpret this as evidence of being 'strong' or 'feisty', but many people prefer to steer clear of an aggressive individual. Unlike the passive person whose anger is covert, the aggressive person's anger is overt – there's nothing hidden about it.

Examples of an aggressive approach in a relationship would be one partner using 'put-down' language when addressing the other – "You're awful", "you're just lazy", "you're talking a load of nonsense", "you're horrible", "you're stupid", "you're wrong!" This is aggressive language, and while the language may not always be as direct, the aim is the same – to put down the other. Aggressive people seem to have a need to always be right, which of course means somebody else must always be wrong.

So what is it that makes some people aggressive? In some cases it can be learned behaviour – "my mother was like this." The more likely explanation is that they find the experience of intimidating others to be enjoyable and therefore worth doing. For a long time all bullies were thought to have low self-esteem, putting others down to try to make themselves feel bigger than they really feel inside. But recent studies looking at bullying in schools suggest that bullies like to put others down simply because they can, that they actually have quite strong self-esteem and like to power it over others in an intimidating way. My own observations tend to support this latter view. Aggressive people often do see themselves as being at the top of the pecking order and try to keep it that way by inducing fear in others. This might seem rather primitive and socially immature, but the typical bully often has an under-developed sense of empathy for others' sufferings, which makes it easy for them to be openly aggressive.

Passive-Aggressive Mode

Passivity and aggression can sometimes be combined. Somebody may seem passive, giving the appearance of going along with things, but in the background they are doing their best to sabotage whatever it is they are supposed to be supporting. This is known as being passive-aggressive. What you see is not what you get. They want to be approved of and to be seen as co-operating, but conflicting emotions caused by agreeing to do something they really don't want to do can make it hard for them. As a consequence, the damage is carried out quietly in the background.

An example of this would be a husband inviting his mother to lunch and his wife not being happy about this, but instead of voicing her feelings, the wife sabotages the situation by making sure that the date of the visit coincides with something else. This makes her look innocent and co-operative, but in reality she has been deceitful and unkind to both her husband and mother-in-law.

Assertive Mode

Being assertive means using a style of communicating that's constructive and clear, without being aggressive. If you don't agree with something, you have the choice to speak up about it or decide it's not really worth speaking up about. By contrast, passive people feel they have no choice but to always let it go, to say nothing even when they don't agree with something.

Sometimes there's a fine line between speaking up and just letting something go. The fact is that some things really aren't worth speaking up about. I once knew a woman who was so overly assertive she would take a stand on every little thing, which of course made it uncomfortable for people to be around her. For example, if anybody sat in her chair when visiting, she would (respectfully) ask them to move. Although she was being assertive, I believe this type of situation wouldn't be worth bothering with, unless perhaps she could only get physically comfortable sitting in that particular chair. But that wasn't the case with this woman.

Assertiveness means expressing negative and positive feelings in a constructive way, being able to say no and to make requests of others without feeling guilty, asking questions and expressing opinions (regardless of others having opposing views). In short, using your voice in an assertive way puts you on the playing field of life.

Learning to Become Assertive

Being assertive is a learned skill. If you are uncomfortable around speaking up for yourself or expressing how you feel, you just need to follow a particular formula. It might feel a bit mechanical at first, but others won't know you are engaging in a process. Once you become more confident expressing yourself in an assertive way, it will begin to feel more natural.

Expressing Negative Feelings

From my observations over the years, people tend to find expressing their negative feelings to others the most difficult part of being assertive. Expressing how you feel about somebody's behaviour simply involves following a five-part formula which includes the following steps:

- Gaining attention
- The sweetener
- Naming the behaviour
- The impact of that behaviour on you
- The request for change

Julie came to see me because she was unhappy with the way things were heading in her marriage. In the evenings when her husband Keith arrived home from work, he would go straight to the fridge for a can of beer and then sit down in front of the TV to unwind. This behaviour left Julie feeling invisible and unloved. When asking her how she would like Keith to be when he came home, Julie said that she wanted him to at least acknowledge her, to say hello, maybe kiss her, ask how her day has been, and for him to also acknowledge their ten-month-old baby boy Jayden.

When I asked Julie why she hadn't been able to discuss her needs with her husband, she explained that Keith had been having a stressful time at work lately, so she didn't want to upset him by pointing out how his behaviour at home was making her feel. This is an example of how a passive person puts another's needs before their own. The Fortune Telling thinking error is also in action here with Julie assuming that Keith would be upset if she talked to him about his behaviour. Julie and I created a plan for her to try a more assertive approach with Keith. The aim was for her to tell Keith how his aloof behaviour was upsetting her and how she would like him to be instead.

Usually we can choose when and where to discuss a problem with our partners. We can make it 'hot off the press' by mentioning the behaviour as it's occurring or we can 'set the scene' and choose a time we think would be best. This might be when the person is in a good mood or when you are alone together. Bringing issues up at inappropriate times such as when sitting in a restaurant with friends would obviously be disrespectful to your partner and to others too. Julie intended to speak to Keith after dinner that evening when the baby was asleep. Before following the formula for expressing negative emotions, Julie first needed to get Keith's attention.

Gaining Attention: Julie's plan to gain Keith's attention so that he actually listened to her was as follows. Face-to-face, she would request him to turn the TV off for a moment, and then say "Keith, there's something important that I want to talk to you about, I'd really like you to listen, then we can talk about it together."

Sweetener: Sweeteners are statements that show understanding and soften the impact of what's to come, such as "I know you're quite stressed at the moment" or "You might not realise it." There are times when a sweetener is not appropriate, but it's usually helpful as a good 'softening' strategy. The sweetener Julie planned to use was "Keith, you probably don't realise it, but..."

Naming the Behaviour: This comes straight after the sweetener. When being assertive, the focus is always on the behaviour, not on putting the person down. Julie would need to be specific with the behaviour that she finds upsetting. If she expressed it in general terms – "you're always ignoring me" – then that would probably put Keith on the defensive and an argument could easily develop. Being quite specific, Julie aimed to say "each night when you come home, when you walk past me and Jayden, and then sit down with your beer to watch TV..." This is naming the specific behaviour that is upsetting Julie.

Describe the Impact of the Behaviour: After naming the behaviour, the next part of the sequence is to describe the emotional impact that particular behaviour is having on you. This might be feeling annoyed, frustrated, disappointed, confused, let down or whatever it is that you're experiencing. Julie wanted to describe how Keith's behaviour makes her feel unimportant so she intended to say "I just want you to know that I feel like I'm invisible, as though I'm not very important in your life. I feel unloved."

The Request: It's important to complete your assertiveness statement with a specific request. Simply tell the person what you want. Julie wanted Keith to acknowledge her when he came home from work. What she planned to say was "I'd really appreciate it if when you come home, you just say hello, give me a little kiss and a hug, ask me how my day's been, say hello to Jayden and acknowledge that we're your little family, so we can feel that we're important to you."

If we look at Julie's plan to express her negative feelings to Keith, you can see that using the assertiveness formula is a powerful tool. Julie isn't putting Keith down at any personal level and what she is saying is presented in a respectful and caring way. When using this strategy to express negative feelings, once you have completed what you want to say, simply look at the person and wait for a response. If no response is forthcoming, you can say "Well, what do you think of that?" This puts the ball in their court as you wait for some acknowledgement. Usually there is an apology, and when this happens, allow them some time to open up if they want to without interrupting. Then say thank you for their acknowledging the issue you raised and watch for the behavioural changes to begin taking place.

You might wonder why Julie wasn't more proactive in greeting Keith in the way she would like to be greeted when he came home – giving him a kiss and a hug, and asking him about *his* day. As passive people prefer to avoid confrontation, they may also avoid taking the initiative. They tend to wait for things to happen to them and then respond. In Julie's case, raising her issue with Keith also allowed *him* to open up about how he was feeling. He had, in fact, been feeling a bit unloved himself as Julie hadn't seemed very interested in him. Keith was also displaying passive characteristics by bottling up how he was feeling and if Julie had remained in her passive state, then it's very likely the quality of their relationship would have continued to deteriorate. As a result of their discussion, Keith's behaviour on arriving home did change, providing them both with the warmth and emotional connection they wanted.

Dealing with Interruptions

Let's now look at some things that can go wrong when you attempt to express negative feelings in an assertive way to your partner. For example, what if your partner interrupts you before you have finished speaking? When this happens, make a hand gesture like a halt sign to show you haven't yet finished and say "could you please hear me out", then continue with what you are saying. If you are interrupted a second time, while raising your hand again, repeat in a slightly firmer tone "could you please respect me enough to hear me out." If there is a further inter-ruption, place your halt signal more in the middle so that you block your partner's face from view and repeat for one last time "I'm asking that you listen to me, can you please hear me out, then you can say what you want to say once I'm finished." If your partner continues to interrupt or walks away, then you are faced with a problem involving a lack of respect in your relationship. Without respect, developing open and honest communication is likely to be difficult.

Using Bridging Phrases

Once you have stated your 'issue' using the assertiveness approach, make sure you aren't manipulated into deviating from your particular topic. For example, your partner tries to take you down a different path by saying something such as "well what about when you did... last week?" When this happens, it's important that you don't get drawn into defending yourself over some other issue. Stay with what you were discussing. You can use a bridging phrase such as "Whether that's true or not" and then return to naming the specific behaviour you are trying to address ("when you...") and continue with what you were saying. Other bridging phrases are "Regardless of that" or "Nevertheless". Use one of these two phrases if an excuse is being given as to why the unwanted behaviour occurs. Be more succinct in repeating your sequence if you have to go back to the start, so that it's just naming the behaviour, its impact on you, and your request about how you want things to be. There's no need to repeat your sweetener if you aren't being listened to in a respectful way.

Using the assertive style of communicating means you don't bottle up negative emotions. You may not always get what you want, but at least the issue is out 'on the table' as a problem to be solved rather than building up inside you.

Expressing Positive Feelings

Some people feel inhibited about expressing how they feel, even when what they want to say is of a positive nature. In a relationship, opportunities for expressing positive emotions are like gifts. For example, when Julie's husband treats her in the way she wants to be treated (acknowledging her in a loving way), then this is an opportunity for Julie to express positive feelings to Keith. She could say something along the lines of "I really love it when you do this" so that Keith is in no doubt that what he is doing is appreciated.

Giving positive feedback to others can reinforce the desired behaviour. Some people might view this as manipulation, but being open about what you like and don't like is good communication, especially within a relationship situation. Using positive reinforcement (saying when something pleases you) combined with expressing negative feelings when something displeases you is known as 'shaping'. You can shape a person's behaviour by simply expressing how you feel. It's a bit like training a dog. If the dog does something you like, and you want this behaviour repeated, then praising the dog will positively reinforce the dog's actions. If the dog is doing something you don't like, using your voice in a disapproving way will let the dog know that this behaviour is not wanted. Although communicating with humans is not as simple as training dogs, the principle remains the same. By providing both positive and negative feedback, you can shape the desired behaviour of your partner.

Moving from the relationship context to the work environment, research shows the number one motivating factor for people at work is being recognised and acknowledged for a job well done. If supervisors and managers want a motivated workforce, then they need to look at providing positive feedback that is sincere, timely and warranted.

Additionally, the language used when giving somebody positive feedback needs to be appropriate. I remember a manager who used to describe just about everything that anyone did as being "brilliant!" From the secretary who brought him a cup of coffee to the sales rep who happened to clinch a sought-after deal for the company, it was all "absolutely brilliant!" There was no discriminating between actions. Was this manager providing positive feedback that was motivating his staff? Although better than no feedback at all, too much "brilliant" feedback from this man may have not meant much for those on the receiving end. Although perhaps well meaning, the expression would have become devalued by being used so often and for so little, revealing more than anything, a limitation or laziness in this man's use of the English language.

Saying No Without Feeling Guilty

If you have a healthy level of intimacy in your relationship, you are likely to feel free to be yourself, which makes it easier to decline requests from your partner without feeling guilty. However, in any relationship, some degree of give and take is often the norm, which means making compromises now and again and expecting them in return. For example, if you love to go to the opera but your partner doesn't like opera, then you can either go alone or with a friend, or you can ask your partner to come along especially for you. Alternatively, your partner might love football, a sport that leaves you cold, but for the sake of the relationship, now and again, you compromise your wants and go along just for him or her, if that's what they have requested.

There are those who say 'compromise' is a dirty word, and that by compromising nobody really gets what they want. That might have an element of truth to it, but it's not really about going to the opera or going to watch football, it's all about pleasing your partner now and again at your own expense. If you want a healthy and happy relationship built on intimacy, then you would occasionally choose to engage in such activities because compromise can increase the quality of your relationship. Compromise in a relationship (depending, of course, on the nature of the request) is like an act of kindness that demonstrates caring.

If you are really digging your toes in and declining your partner's requests all the time, then perhaps you need to ask yourself – is this creating intimacy for our relationship? Certainly you might be acting true to yourself, but when in a partnership, compromise now and again is important. If you have a strong intimate relationship, this will be easy for both of you. If you don't, then there could be daily battles to fight, a situation not conducive to the happiness of either party.

Moving outside of the relationship context, how many times do you want to decline somebody's request, but hear yourself saying the opposite, and then feel angry with yourself and angry with the person who made the request? This is an example of being passive, feeling as though you have no choice but to say yes. You might try to avoid saying yes by making an excuse, but sometimes this approach backfires and you end up with the unwanted task anyway.

Kirsten was asked by a neighbour if she would take on the role of secretary for a committee which required her attending meetings every Tuesday evening. Kirsten hated committees and really didn't want to take this on, but found herself saying "I'd love to do it, but I can't because I have some other commitment on Tuesdays, so sorry about that." This excuse didn't deter the rather pushy neighbour as she then suggested that the committee meetings could change to Wednesday evenings especially to accommodate Kirsten. This left Kirsten feeling that she had no option but to accept, so while pretending to be pleased, she was furious inside.

Kirsten needed to be able to decline her neighbour's request in a respectful but firm way, which would mean exercising assertiveness. For example, when asked if she would take on the role of secretary for the committee, Kirsten could have simply said "Thanks for asking me, but I'm sorry, I'm going to have to say no to that." If the pressure comes on with the pushy neighbour saying "oh but there's nobody else, and you'd be so good at doing that", Kirsten would need to 'stick to her guns' by simply repeating her reply. There's no need to feel guilty about refusing to do something you don't want to do. It's your right to decline or accept based on what you want to do. Some people love being on committees, but to others they are anathema. If you really feel you need to provide an excuse to help you to say no, you can always say something along the lines of "Thanks for thinking of me, but I'm really very busy, so will have to say no to that."

Sometimes we do agree to take on things when we would rather not, but that's all part of life. It's the emotional conse-quences that determine whether you are harming yourself by being consistently passive. Having pent-up anger and resentment is not good for your body, and if you are stewing emotionally, then you may need to have a good look at who is running your life and why it doesn't seem to be you. When you think about it, there are plenty of people declining other people's requests all the time, so why shouldn't you do the same?

Making Requests Without Feeling Guilty

Sometimes we want to simply make a request without any need to express negative feelings. This usually involves using a sweetener and the request. As with feeling bad about saying no, some people feel awkward or guilty about making requests, even within their relationships. If we are to feel free to be ourselves, then there's no need for any undue discomfort about making a request. In a truly intimate relationship, making a request of your partner would feel emotionally 'safe'. However, for relationships lacking intimacy, this could create some anxiety or guilt.

Jane came to see me because she had been feeling a bit down about being overlooked for a promotion at work. Her partner (Mark) was currently going through a stressful time in his job, which made it difficult for Jane to ask for some physical and emotional comfort from him. When I asked Jane why she couldn't just go and put her arms around Mark, letting her body make the request for a hug, Jane told me that if she did that, Mark would interpret this as a sexual invitation.

Unfortunately, I hear this same story many times. One partner (usually the woman) wants to be cuddled and hugged but her partner (usually the man) interprets this as an invitation for sex. Imagine the patterns of behaviour that could develop given this misinterpretation of needs. The woman starts to avoid any physical contact because she believes it will only be viewed in a sexual context by her partner, thereby causing him to feel rejected. But she too feels rejected because her partner is not giving her the physical tenderness she wants without it becoming sexualised.

In this situation, honest verbal communication is really important. Although couples may have differing sexual libidos, the natural consequence of physical affection between two consenting adults is sex. Sex is natural, but for many people in this busy world it has become the last task to perform before going to sleep. Intimacy is based on qualities such as respect, open communication and natural affection, and Jane would need to use her voice as well as her body to make a request of Mark. She could do this by stating as a sweetener, "You've probably had a stressful day too", then she could make her request, "but right now, I'd really appreciate a hug, I just want to be held in your arms and feel comforted because I've had a really disappointing day at work." Jane would then physically embrace Mark. If Mark were to try to progress from a cuddle to sexual caressing, then Jane would need to restate her request "Right now Mark, I just want to be comforted by having a cuddle, I don't want sex, just a cuddle." This message clearly states what Jane wants, and even if Mark develops an erection from the cuddle, Jane is still entitled to a non-sexual cuddle without feeling she has to go any further.

Mark could continue hugging Jane, even if he did have an erection. Like anxiety symptoms, erections eventually disappear if they are ignored for long enough!

Mark and Jane both required some therapy to help with their communication styles and their expectations of each other in their relationship. By working on emotional intimacy, sex eventually became more natural and conflict-free for both of them.

Let's now look at an example of making requests without feeling guilty in a workplace situation. Sue came to see me because she was feeling really out of her depth in a new supervisory position at work. Having a more passive than assertive approach, Sue believed that if she treated her staff in a kind and friendly way, then they wouldn't cause her much trouble. She couldn't have been more wrong. To be in a position of responsibility for others, you need good assertiveness skills as, unfortunately, there are always those who will take advantage of somebody with a passive nature.

One of Sue's team members began repeatedly turning up for work fifteen minutes late. Sue worried about mentioning the tardy behaviour to the woman for fear of upsetting her. As well as this, other managers were continually putting pressure on Sue to take on extra responsibilities, even though she was already over-loaded in her current role. As a consequence of these situations, Sue began suffering from anxiety. Each morning getting ready for work, she felt nauseous and tense, and the sense of pride she had experienced on being promoted was now gone. A passive supervisor or manager may be liked and popular with staff, but more often than not they are not respected, people take advantage of their good nature.

During the therapy sessions, we looked at how Sue could be more assertive by making requests. This involved her asking the tardy team member to arrive on time and for the pushy managers to stop pressuring her to take on more work. After role-playing both these situations during the therapy session, Sue made her requests at work in an assertive manner and with good results.

Making requests of others means exercising good self-care. When we practice being more assertive, a surprising thing happens. Rather than being disapproved of by others, we actually become more respected and held in higher esteem because of it. For Sue, life at work became much easier once she started using a more assertive approach and the anxiety she was experiencing each morning gradually disappeared.

Expressing Opinions

We all have our own particular way of viewing things, and this is what makes life interesting, because it creates stimulating conversation and debate. Even when nobody agrees with you, expressing your opinions is important and demonstrates healthy self-esteem. We all have a right to our opinions and we all have a voice with which to express them.

In a relationship, expressing opinions is a good way of really getting to know each other. If you don't like or don't agree with what your partner is saying, it's healthy to debate it in a respectful way. If you still have completely opposing views, then there's no point in continuing the "you're wrong, I'm right" standoff. In this situation it is far better to be gracious and just let it go. To turn differing opinions into an aggressive no-win argument is destructive behaviour. Remember it's quite civilised to 'agree to differ' and, as the French might say, "Vive la difference!"

> *I do not agree with what you have to say, but I'll defend to the death your right to say it.*
> Voltaire

Chapter Ten

Emotions and Relationships

One of the most emotionally rewarding things we humans can experience during our time on Earth is to share a loving healthy relationship with another person. Research shows that a happy marital relationship correlates with good health and longevity. Unfortunately, many marriages now don't last long enough for a couple to even reach old age together, a common reason for this being the failure of emotional intimacy being developed in the relationship.

The emotional power generated when we fall in love can have a huge impact on every aspect of our being, and not always for the best. Some of the most destructive elements of human behaviour can be found in the realm of romantic relationships. This chapter looks at how we can develop and maintain emotional intimacy in relationships.

Emotional Intimacy

If you are in a relationship, how well do you really know and understand your partner? There's a little exercise that I sometimes ask couples to do which involves each pretending to be the other for a few hours. This exercise can produce some powerful insights into how well each partner actually knows the other. It's also a good indicator of how much emotional intimacy is operating within the relationship.

When unhappy couples come to see me for relationship therapy, the most common cause of their unhappiness is their failure to have developed real intimacy. Even though a couple may have been together for many years, if their relationship is lacking in emotional intimacy, then they might just as well be flatmates.

So what is intimacy? Many people assume that I'm talking about physical intimacy when I ask them to describe the level of intimacy in their relationship. To have a deep, loving and lasting relationship you need a lot more than just sex. Sex is only one of the many components that make up intimacy. Life-long intimacy is based on emotions more than anything else, and if the emotional balance is right, then the physical balance is usually right too. To my mind, emotional intimacy between two people involves a variety of qualities such as respect, companionship, affection (both physical and verbal), open communication, compatibility, trust, honesty, kindness and shared values. It also involves a feeling of being special to each other, knowing that in the eyes of your partner, you are the special 'other', that you are on each other's side in the world.

There are now so many people ending their relationships far too easily. By having emotional intimacy as the gel holding the relationship together, there are few reasons why couples shouldn't still value and enjoy being with each other right up to old age – 'until death us do part'. When real-life difficulties arise, such as serious illness or financial hardship, a relationship built on emotional intimacy is worth its weight in gold, whereas a relationship based on physical appearance, expedience, status, worldly 'success' or material gain is likely to crumble when faced with life's more difficult challenges.

The following pages provide a detailed account of what I believe to be the main ingredients we need to develop a loving and lasting intimate relationship. This list is based on my clinical observations with clients as well as from my own personal relationships. You might consider some of these qualities a bit old-fashioned, but to my mind, they not only create emotional intimacy within a relationship, they also maintain and strengthen it, enabling the relationship to last the course.

Respect

Let's start with respect, a quality that now seems to be such an out-dated concept, yet it's one of the key elements missing in modern-day relationships. So what does having respect for somebody else mean? To my mind, respect is all about valuing each other, being courteous and considerate in how you treat each other, and considering the feelings and needs of your partner because of the high value you place on them. Your feelings of respect are demonstrated by your verbal interaction and behaviour.

The opposite of respect is a lack of regard or consideration, manifesting in indifference or even contempt. To disrespect is to disregard the other, to treat them as though this person's feelings are of no significant value, even though they are your partner. Some people say that respect has to be earned, but I believe this is nonsense. More often than not, this idea is utilised as an excuse for somebody to continue behaving in a way that is upsetting their partner. The fact that somebody has made the decision to be your partner out of all the millions of people on the planet is in itself worthy of some respect, unless of course, they are *deliberately* harming you emotionally or physically, in which case the relationship may not be worth repairing.

In our everyday work environment, we often need to deal with customers or clients, and we are expected to treat them with respect, because if we don't, they are likely to take their custom elsewhere. So obviously, it's in our best interests to treat customers or clients in this way, it makes good sense. It's equally important that we treat our partners with respect. We are, after all, free agents (in most of the developed world at least), and we don't have to stay in relationships we don't want to be in, therefore, the person you have chosen to be with and who has chosen to be with you, is worthy of respect. If you have respect for yourself, then it's easy to respect your partner and the relationship you have with each other.

Natural Affection

When affection is frequently expressed both physically and verbally between partners, it's a good sign that the relationship is healthy. Being naturally affectionate means you just can't help wanting to touch your partner as you walk past them in the kitchen, or give them a spontaneous hug or kiss, or tell them (just out of the blue) how much you love them. There's nothing forced about it, in fact, it's something that you can't help doing, which is why it's called *natural* affection. It creates emotional warmth as well as an element of playfulness.

I'm going to include sex in this Natural Affection category because in an intimate adult relationship, touching each other naturally leads to sex. That's as nature intended it. However, I'm referring to sexual interaction which is part of an emotional connection between two people in a relationship as opposed to casual sex between people who are virtually strangers.

There's no doubt that we humans complicate our sex lives, adding all manner of ideas and rules about how things should be which, not surprisingly, can lead to performance anxiety. It is, of course, possible to have a close intimate relationship that doesn't involve sex. It might be unusual, but it's certainly possible, especially as people get older when a touch of the hand can represent an expression of deep affection.

I have deliberately not mentioned 'love' in my list of ingredients because I believe that strong natural affection is a good basis for developing real intimacy. Philosophers and poets have spent thousands of years trying to work out what love is without much consensus. I would describe love as a strong positive emotion that is loaded with a special kind of energy. We can love our partners, children, family, friends and pets. It's all much the same feeling, but the intensity of the love can obviously vary.

Feeling 'Safe' to be Yourself

If you don't feel you can be spontaneous in your relationship, then perhaps you don't feel 'safe' enough to really be yourself. In this context, the word 'safe' doesn't involve fear of being physically harmed. To feel emotionally safe means feeling free to be completely spontaneous, to feel free to say the wrong thing, to make a mistake, to be 'thick' now and again, to play, to sing, to dance, to laugh at yourself. In other words, to be human without fear of being looked down upon, disapproved of or judged by your partner.

Being in an intimate relationship is like coming home and putting on a comfortable pair of slippers or even going barefoot. You feel very compatible and easy with each other, having no need to be anything other than who you are. Such an emotionally secure state allows honesty and openness to occur naturally because you feel okay about being authentically you. You feel more 'at home' with this other person than you do with anybody else in the world. If you can't relax with your partner because you can't be seen without makeup or the right clothes, or you don't express your opinions because your partner might not approve, then you probably need to ask yourself what is going on. For intimacy to develop in a relationship, it's important that you can both be your true selves, and enjoy being like this, knowing that your partner loves you for who you really are.

Feeling Special

Feeling that you are special to your partner is an important element in an intimate relationship. Even when you are on the other side of the world, thousands of miles away from each other, you still feel special because of that unique bond you have with each other. You think about each other and miss being together. You know that of the millions of people on our planet, this other human being is connected to you in a very special way.

There are so many clients who come to see me for couple therapy because they don't feel special in their relationship. Interestingly, the majority of these clients are women. If you don't feel as though you are very special to your partner, do you know why? It may be that he or she *does* regard you as being special, but they aren't demonstrating it with words or actions. If this is the case, what can you do about it? Perhaps you aren't letting them know what they could say or do to make you feel special. Too many people fall into the trap of believing they shouldn't have to ask their partner to make them feel special because "if he really loved me, it would already be happening." But not everybody is emotionally competent, and plenty of people (often males) need some guidance as to how they can go about demonstrating their love towards their partner.

In order to initiate any change in this area, you first need to know what you do or don't want. You then need to know how to ask for your needs to be met. This is where good communication is valuable. From my experience, most women don't want a bunch of flowers or a piece of jewellery to make them feel special in a relationship, more than anything else they want the emotional warmth of intimacy with their partner.

Being on Each Other's Side

Being on each other's side could be described as 'couple solidarity'. In the face of adversity, you stick up for each other. When somebody is trying to put your partner down (even if what they are saying seems to be true), you take your partner's side because it is your partner, your special mate who is being slighted or insulted. It's one of those situations when you *can* take it personally, you're batting for your significant other in the big world, you are on each other's side like a close-knit family.

In situations when you and your partner are disagreeing over something, you can still practice being on each other's side. Why not let him or her win now and again, even when you know they are wrong, why not let them be right? You don't have to take a stand on every little thing. So if he or she changes the way you stacked the dishwasher, well, so what? If you can't bear to let them be right because they are so wrong, you can always 'agree to disagree' but still be supportive of each other. If you do want to make an issue over something, make sure it's something worthwhile, an issue worth pursuing rather than some trivial detail.

Shared Values

Values are those things we hold in high esteem, things that are so important to us, we wouldn't want to compromise our position within those areas. Therefore, being compatible by sharing common values is a helpful ingredient for a good relationship. Caring for family and friends, honesty, monogamy, a strong work ethic, thrift, self-sufficiency, spirituality, education, travel, community service and healthy living are all examples of things that we might hold as values.

If a couple share the same values, then the relationship is likely to fare better than if they have opposing values. Imagine the difficulty of a situation if one partner suddenly wants to try recreational drugs or decides to take up smoking, whereas the other partner places a high value on being healthy, or if one person wants to have extra-marital affairs when their partner values a faithful monogamous relationship. Obviously these types of situations have the potential to destroy a relationship which makes it a wise move to really get to know your partner well before making any commitment. Having opposing values can really undermine a relationship, however, if there's a strong sense of mutual respect and kindness operating, it would be unusual to want affairs or to start smoking, knowing that this would upset the most important person in your world.

Trust

Sometimes when a person has been deeply hurt or let down in the past by somebody they loved and trusted, the negative emotional consequence of that experience can cause them to be generally mistrustful and suspicious in new relationships, to feel as though they are just waiting for the next inevitable betrayal. In an intimate relationship, there is only room for trust. Even when your current partner has let you down in the past, if they have expressed regret over this and learned from it, then I believe for the sake of the relationship, it's best for you to exercise trust. If you trust your partner, then you believe what they tell you, you take it at face value. This makes for an easy life as you don't need to monitor or fret about them being 'up to no good' behind your back. When people betray trust, it's often a case of real intimacy having been missing in the relationship anyway, certainly the ingredients of respect and honesty.

Some people who have been betrayed in the past by their partners are reluctant to let down their guard and trust again, claiming that "a leopard can't change its spots." But we are human beings not leopards, and we can and do change our behaviour. Most people don't initiate affairs with the intent of upsetting their partners, and I know of many instances in which the first betrayal was the one and only, with a harsh lesson learned from that experience.

Imagine what it would be like to have your husband or wife mistrusting you, checking on your every move and watching your every interaction with others. Suspicion can create an atmosphere in which respect is impossible and impedes any demonstrations of natural affection. Trust in a relationship is a necessity if emotional intimacy is to develop.

Shared Activities
Spending time engaging in shared activities can help in maintaining emotional intimacy as external stimuli provide opportunities for differing opinions, debate, humour and ideas, all of which involve really getting to know each other. Sharing a hobby together, seeing a movie or dining out now and again are important, especially when you become parents, as it's so easy to

lose track of who you are as a couple. I see too many people who become so caught up with their parenting (or career roles), they forget to work on the intimacy aspect of their relationship. Spending some 'couple time' away from the children to maintain romantic intimacy together or to catch up on social contact with friends is not only good for the parents, it's also good for the children. It expands a child's view of mum and dad, seeing them as being special to each other as well as social beings who interact with others outside of the family unit.

Individual Activities

It can also be emotionally healthy to have individual interests as well as shared interests. Intimacy is being close, but not so close that you are suffocating each other in a co-dependent situation. To have the freedom to pursue a hobby or pastime as an individual without your partner can be beneficial. Having individual interests often strengthens intimacy as they provide opportunities for gaining self-confidence in different areas and bringing new topics of conversation into the relationship.

I once knew a woman whose husband was so possessive of her that he sat outside in the car while she attended a Tupperware party. This was the condition he placed on her being allowed out if she wanted to go anywhere as an individual. Needless to say, this relationship (which was mainly based on fear and control) didn't last.

Kindness

To be kind to your partner involves a gentle unassuming type of caring, performing spontaneous acts of kindness without any requirement that they be acknowledged or reciprocated. And we do this simply because that person is our dearest and best friend, our soulmate. Kindness is often associated with a spiritual element, its whole motive being to give without expectation of anything in return. And it's the same in the relationship sphere, we are kind because we want to be, and such behaviour, especially when it's mutual, makes for a pleasant and caring home environment.

Constant kindness can accomplish much. As the sun makes ice melt, kindness causes misunderstanding, mistrust and hostility to evaporate.
Albert Schweitzer

Using Communication to Build Lasting Intimacy

Good communication is vital for the development and maintenance of intimacy. If people don't feel special, loved or respected in their relationship, they won't see a lot of point in communicating this to a partner who appears not to care much anyway, so nothing is said. But it's important that you do speak up, because many partners who are perceived as being unloving actually do care, they just don't know how to break the patterns that may have developed. It could be that once the honeymoon period was over, they just settled into imitating their parents' models of what a marriage is supposed to be like, and those behaviours became habits, which over time became the norm.

Many, many times I have heard people (mostly men) say that they were not aware of how unhappy their partners were. In fact, they were under the impression that everything was fine. Then one day out of the blue, their partner decides they want to end the relationship, leaving the other to wonder why the unhappiness had never been mentioned, which of course, would have provided some opportunity for problem solving and possible change.

One of the saddest things in these cases is that the partner who has been left has not learned anything other than that he can't trust appearances anymore. If a new partner appears happy and contented, well so did the previous one, even though she wasn't. In my view, it's really unfair to 'pull the plug' on a relationship without any communication in regard to perceived problems, to not even give your partner a chance. If you have both worked on building strong emotional intimacy in your relationship, then that relationship is in a healthy state to overcome most of life's stormy periods, and talking about problems, no matter how sensitive or painful, needs to be the first course of action.

Romantic Liaisons

Nature has programmed us to feel romantically and sexually attracted to each other, and of course, there is obviously good evolutionary value in this for the continuation of the human species. Acting on these romantic inclinations can result in wonderful emotional highs, but unfortunately, there's also a lot of scope for heartbreak.

Falling in Love

Over twenty years ago, a colleague of mine (Sarah) was diagnosed with a particularly aggressive form of cancer. The hospital advised this thirty-seven-year-old woman that she had only about six months to live. Sarah was devastated by the diagnosis but decided she still felt well enough to fulfil one of her life's ambitions. She had never been to the South Island of New Zealand, so she wasted no time in purchasing her airline ticket. If you don't know what New Zealand's South Island is like, imagine something between the Swiss Alps and Yosemite National Park. In short, it's a very grand and extremely beautiful place.

Nine months later, when Sarah returned from her holiday, she was in good health and all trace of the cancer had disappeared. It may be that touring around the South Island had contributed to her miraculous cure, or that the chemotherapy treatment had helped, but during her time away something totally unexpected happened to Sarah. She met a new man when visiting the city of Christchurch and fell instantly and madly in love with him. He had a motorbike and wanted to tour the South Island too, so Sarah completed the rest of her trip on the back of his bike.

Falling in love is a tremendously powerful emotion which can have a hugely positive impact on the body. I suspect that this was a main contributor to Sarah's complete recovery. I met her again recently and she is still cancer-free, although the new relationship didn't work out that well after all. Describing her trip to the South Island all those years ago, Sarah said she felt like "a dizzy teenage girl, completely over the moon in love."

If you have ever felt 'over the moon in love', you will know what a powerful emotion it is. The Norwegians call this euphoric feeling 'forelsket', which means a type of madness, a time when all the hormones in your body are going crazy. Others have described falling in love as being like a conflagration, which means burning like a large destructive fire. A strong emotion such as this can impact forcefully on our thoughts and physiology as well as on our behaviour. However, the passion eventually wears off and if the relationship is healthy, a deep love based on real intimacy begins to develop.

In the wrong situation, of course, the crazy passionate feeling of falling in love can create mayhem, resulting in some regrettable decisions and a lot of heartache. There are many clients who complain about loving their partners but not being *in love* with them. This 'being in love' they refer to is that conflagration state, an overwhelming desire to be with the idolised other. There's no doubt that it's an extremely powerful feeling, nature's ploy to get two people together to copulate in the hope of creating new people. Unfortunately, nature is not that bothered whether a person is married to another, or whether they already have a family. Once a person is emotionally smitten, it creates an imperative that has the potential to destroy existing family units and hurt a lot of people.

There are those who become addicted to the emotional 'high' that falling in love can bring. As though under the influence of a powerful drug, they spend their whole lives moving from one relationship to another. As the fire of the current love dies down, it can only be rekindled by a new love, and so real intimacy with the one person is never given a chance to develop. When I see these clients, I suggest that they focus all their energy on developing emotional intimacy with their current partner, as long as the two people are compatible and have feelings of affection for each other, and that the relationship has a healthy enough foundation.

Extramarital Affairs

If two people come to see me wanting help with building intimacy in their relationship, and I know there's an extramarital affair continuing in the background, then I have to tell them that relationship therapy tends to work best when it's for two people. If a third party remains on the scene while the couple are trying to repair their marriage, then there's little chance of success because intimacy can't thrive in an atmosphere of betrayal.

As human beings, we are going to feel strongly attracted to other people now and again, but this doesn't mean we have to act on that attraction. If you value the relationship you have with your partner, then I would advise you to not even be tempted to participate in an innocent "let's meet for coffee" type of scenario with anybody you feel strongly attracted to. Once that falling in love madness takes hold, people are a lot less able to think clearly and rationally about their current commitments.

The emotional power involved in having an affair can be like a drug and be very difficult to give up. As well as the magical highs, there are usually feelings of guilt combined with conflicting wants, usually to retain both relationships – the one with the spouse as well as with the new lover. But our society doesn't approve of three-way relationships, and nor would the spouse or the new lover, unless of course you have an open marriage. In my time as a therapist though, I have seen enough open marriage situations to conclude that they rarely bring true happiness.

Although there are plenty of people who 'accidentally' fall in love, resulting in an affair, there are those who deliberately cheat, seeking out affairs and hoping their behaviour remains undetected by the spouse. However, it's usually just a matter of time before the new love wants more than to simply stay in the background. When demands for evidence of a commitment are voiced by the new love, the cheating partner often claims that this is, of course, what they want too, but the time just isn't quite right yet. In this situation, it's often a case of one person preferring to keep the status quo (having their lover and their spouse) as long as the spouse doesn't know and the new love doesn't 'rock the boat'. When the lover becomes more insistent, he or she may suddenly be 'dropped' by the person who they believe is in love with them. In these cases, the affair is more about physical attraction or having a bit of excitement on the side. In this triangular no-win situation, the missing factor in both marriage and affair is emotional intimacy.

In some cases, because the person having the affair doesn't want to be the one that ends the marriage, they begin to find fault with their spouses. Small short-comings are turned into major incidents. For example, if the betrayed spouse happens to mention something they don't like, then this is construed as being 'controlling' by the partner who is having the affair. It's as though the cheating partner is looking for any reason to justify breaking up, and in the process, to make it appear as though the innocent spouse is the problem. This, of course, is grossly unfair, leaving the innocent partner feeling very confused as to why they are suddenly being treated so unreasonably. The aim is to make life so miserable for the unwanted partner that they decide to leave. If this were an employment situation it would be tantamount to 'constructive dismissal'. Things are hurtful enough for the betrayed partner without having all the blame heaped onto them when in fact the marriage is being destroyed by their unfaithful and inconsiderate spouse.

If you are one of those unfortunate souls who have fallen head over heels in love with somebody else, yet can't bear the thought of leaving your spouse or breaking up your family, then you have a big problem. You and probably quite a few others are heading for major heartache, whatever decision comes next. I have seen so many people in emotional agony when they are in these situations. They are literally unable to choose which route to go. It's not a case of their heart saying one thing and their head another. Their heart is split both ways, they don't want to lose either of the people they love most in the world, nor, if there are children, do they want to break up their family.

Sooner or later though, a choice needs to be made. If the choice involves leaving the spouse, the ensuing turmoil can be huge. The rejected spouse often feels devastated. The feelings of rejection and betrayal can last for the rest of their life. A common result of this is future 'commitment phobia', especially for those who had no idea of what had been going on. Not only did they lose half their house and possessions, full access to their children and the spouse they loved, they couldn't find any way in which they could learn from it as they didn't see it coming. Hence, their new approach to future relationships is to protect themselves both emotionally and financially from a similar fate occurring by refusing to make any commitment to a new relationship.

When relationships are broken, children can suffer dreadfully. Family members, including mothers, fathers and siblings, as well as friends of the couple breaking up, all suffer to some degree when one person 'pulls the plug' on their marriage. The house usually needs to be sold and lawyers become involved. The situation creates a ripple-effect of sadness, shock and confusion across the family which gradually turns to bitterness and anger. In short, everybody suffers along with the person wanting to end the relationship. Even years later when things become more settled, feelings of guilt or rejection can continue until death for both the betrayer and the betrayed.

Stab the body and it heals, but injure the heart and the wound lasts a lifetime.
Mineko Iwasaki

If the choice is to break off the affair, allowing a chance for repair and emotional intimacy to develop within the marriage, there is often massive heartbreak here too. Not only will the act of leaving and rejecting the lover feel dreadful, throughout the rest of that person's life, they may wonder if they had made the right choice. If you have ever watched the film *The Bridges of Madison County*, you will appreciate the unfortunate situation of Francesca (played by Meryl Streep) who is about to run off with Robert (the man she has fallen in love with), but at the last minute she chooses to stay with her husband instead. Although she stays right to the end of her life with her husband, her feelings for Robert never leave her. So even though you could say that Francesca did the 'right thing' by putting her family first, the emotional suffering over the loss of Robert continued throughout her remaining years.

My advice to anybody contemplating having a 'harmless affair' with somebody who they feel attracted to and who is attracted to them, is to steer well clear of any romantic or even 'interesting development' if your marriage or relationship is of any value to you. From all the emotional pain I have witnessed over the years, prevention is much, much better than cure. If your marriage is okay but could be better, then work together on building more intimacy. Once emotional intimacy has been developed in the marriage, you will be on steadier ground and be better able to ward off or willingly steer clear of any potential affair situation because you value highly what you already have. If the marriage is cold though, and even with the help of a good therapist there's little hope of it ever being warm and intimate, then it's probably best to end it. At least being separated, you both have the opportunity to find someone more compatible and the chance of a happier life.

There are billions of people in this world and fortunately for us in the more developed countries, we can choose to leave a bad relationship if necessary and seek happiness with somebody else, or aim for a happy single life if we want to. The French philosopher Jean-Paul Sartre claimed that "hell is other people!" In some cases this may be true, but love and joy can also be experienced through other people, especially when we have that special someone with whom we can share our life's journey.

There is no feeling more comforting and consoling than knowing you are right next to the one you love.
(Anonymous)

Chapter Eleven

Spirituality, Philosophy and Our Emotions

To sense that behind anything that can be experienced there is
something that our mind cannot grasp, and whose beauty and
sublimity reaches us only indirectly and as a feeble reflection...
Albert Einstein

Given the conceptual enormity of death, it's understandable that we humans tend to desire some sense of continuity. The idea of there being absolutely nothing else once we die can seem unpalatable for many to accept. It's therefore not surprising that a variety of beliefs have arisen to counteract the finality of life that death apparently represents. This chapter looks at how emotions can play an important and intricate role in our spiritual and philosophical beliefs in relation to mortality and the concept of life continuing in some form after death.

Spirituality

Having a sense of our own spirituality can have nothing to do with any particular religion. Those with a clear religious belief are likely to be living by a set of rules ordained by their God. They accept this to be the truth, trusting their God and the accompanying doctrine. This differs from those who believe in some vague form of a higher power largely based on their own emotional and personal experiences rather than any particular religious doctrine.

During the therapeutic process, the issue of spirituality is often raised. When asked if there really is a God or some advanced higher being (as though a psychologist would have some level of omniscience!), I reply in all honesty that I don't know. I have never had any close encounters of the extraordinary kind, such as a near-death experience involving tunnels and lights, but I do know dozens of people (many of whom had no previous spiritual beliefs) who claim to have experienced this. Whether the 'bright light in the tunnel' phenomenon is of a physical nature (part of the closing down process for the brain when near death) or whether it involves a supernatural element, I don't know. But I do know it can have a profound emotional impact on those who have experienced it, often removing all fear of death.

Those who do hold spiritual beliefs are less likely to fear death than those without any belief in a higher power, as this would obviously provide some sense of meaning to life. Studies show that people who believe in a God generally have better mental and physical well-being than those without any religious faith. Having a spiritual belief can provide emotional comfort for the individual as they journey through this somewhat mysterious process of being born, living an allotted number of days and then dying. Conversely, those religions affirming that hellfire and other extreme forms of horror and torture await unbelievers when they die are likely to create fear for anybody who believed such grisly threats. Such a person could end up very concerned about all those people they love and care for if they thought this might be true, probably spoiling their own enjoyment and happiness in life even though they themselves expect to be 'saved'.

An Emotional Need to Worship

When you look up at the sky on a starry night, what do you make of it all? Do you feel a sense of connection or oneness with the universe, a sense of awe and wonder gazing at that great mysterious mass of twinkling stars that are so far away, we may actually be looking at the past? Or perhaps you don't feel anything at all – it's just the night sky that has always been there, the same old stars and the moon.

The great sense of mystery that some people experience (myself included here) when looking up at a star-filled sky, can bring home the full realisation that here we are, experiencing being alive on this particular planet and nobody *really* knowing how or why we are here. Is it any wonder that throughout the ages and right up to the present time, we humans have had a need to believe in something that explains what life is all about, something that might provide a sense of meaning? We seem to have an innate emotional need to connect with something greater than ourselves, to want a divine parent to look after us, to stay nearby, to help us, to be contactable, and in return for all of this, to be an object of worship. As children we were dependent upon caring adults to help us to survive and to teach us society's 'rules'. For many adults, that longing seems to continue right throughout their lives.

Social animals that live together look to the alpha leaders of their pack or herd for protection and to help with survival, and it can be the same with humans. To look up to somebody we perceive as being a powerful and benevolent guide is reassuring, be that somebody a king or queen, emperor, president, prime minister, religious leader, guru or even dictator – we seem to want a figurehead we can trust to make the right decisions for us, so that we too, like other living creatures might survive.

Fairly recently, there has been some controversy over the discovery of a certain area of the human brain claimed to be responsible for activating spiritual experiences (known as the *God-spot*). Whether this is true or not, I believe that we human beings do tend to have an emotionally-based desire to worship and adore something we perceive to be 'greater' than ourselves, which may explain why we have so many religions in the world. It might also explain why some people are prepared to wait for hours in cold wet weather to catch a glimpse of a celebrity posing and preening on a red carpet or to wave flags and clap as a royal procession goes by. For me, looking up at that twinkling mass of stars in the night sky certainly creates a lot more questions than it does answers.

A Personal Quest for 'The Truth'

Many years ago I set out on a personal quest in search of evidence that would support a paranormal domain existing alongside our everyday world. I was raised in a superstitious household where a parallel universe seemed to exist, mainly manifesting in Good Luck or Bad Luck, and with a variety of 'rituals' used in the hope of influencing these two 'powers'. For example, the act of throwing a pinch of salt over your left shoulder to ward off Bad Luck or hanging up horseshoes as ornaments to attract Good Luck! The idea that there was life after death was a widely held view, a mysterious business for sure, but rarely analysed or discussed in any reasonable way.

Getting back to my quest, partly as a result of my upbringing and partly out of curiosity, I wanted to experience something from which I could say "yes, there is some truth here, I have experienced this myself." My search for the truth involved visiting all manner of people renowned for their extraordinary 'gifts', many claiming to have supernatural powers which gave them access to those beyond the grave. When the people I knew returned full of excitement from their 'sittings' with the gifted ones (spiritualists, mediums, clairvoyants, channellers, fortune tellers), I immediately made my own appointments, the three-month waiting list adding weight to their apparent validity.

In order to properly test these people's claims to being blessed with supernatural abilities, the name I left for each appointment was false. The rationale for this being if I were a charlatan wanting to stage an impressive performance in this field, then the more information I could gather in advance (from a name or phone number), the better the chances of appearing good. If I were a genuinely gifted person, then a customer's name would be of no consequence.

During my meetings with these people, I remained careful not to give away much information about myself. I didn't want them to simply reflect my own statements back to me as proof of their clairvoyant ability. For example, they often wanted to know if somebody in my family had died, and if the answer was yes, then there were more questions about who it was, how and when they died. If nothing was forthcoming that could be used as clues, they often tried taking a different tack by stating very common names and asking me if I knew anybody living or dead by the name of John or Anne!

As my own voice still holds a trace of a Liverpudlian accent, this was quickly seized upon by most of them – "You have people close to you who are far, far away?" Yes, that was correct, but hardly an example of psychic brilliance. The personal messages coming through from the 'other side' were even more futile – "watch your handbag" or "it's important that you eat your greens." Needless to say, this was all very disappointing for somebody hoping for enlightenment on the great mysteries of life, so at the end of each appointment with these individuals, I left with a rising sense of disgust. I hadn't found one shred of evidence to support the fact that any of them possessed extraordinary powers other than to manipulate and impress the gullible. To put it quite bluntly, I found their performances obscene! On the other hand though, if bereaved people are finding some comfort in what they are hearing, even if it is fabrication, then perhaps in some ways these charlatans could be viewed as being more helpful than harmful.

Regardless of my fruitless search for evidence to support life existing within some other dimension after death, I still maintain an open mind to the possibility of there being 'something else'. As mentioned in Chapter Two, the strong feelings of bliss I described are the closest I have ever come to experiencing something that could be described as mystical, but this doesn't necessarily make it spiritual in the true sense of the word. In fact, any strong feelings may simply be a case of falling into the thinking error trap of Emotional Reasoning – "I feel it therefore it must be true." Despite all the 'findings' of my quest, being a psychologist, and working with a variety of people, I believe it is far better to try and maintain an open rather than a closed mind when it comes to the issue of people's spiritual beliefs, simply because spirituality is such an integral and very personal part of being human and as such some sense of respect is warranted.

Becoming More Spiritual

From my observations, more people today seem to be turning to aspects of the Buddhist philosophy to help satisfy their spiritual hunger. According to Buddhist beliefs, as well as being kind and compassionate towards each other, we need to avoid harming other life forms. This all sounds very civilised and appealing, but it does raise some questions on how to combine this philosophy with medical science. For example, in certain situations, by not harming other life forms, we create harm for ourselves. Without human intervention in the form of antibiotics for infectious diseases (typhoid for example), millions of people would not be alive today.

To my mind, one of the most effective ways of developing a sense of your own spirituality is to engage in the daily practice of meditation and mindfulness. Meditation alone can provide a sense of spiritual connection to something bigger than the self, something that is both within us and outside of us. This is how it feels for me anyway, yet I don't know what *it* is, whether it's God, a higher being or simply my own emotional state brought on by the relaxing influence of meditation. Right now though, I'm happy to accept that it's all a great mystery.

Love and Hate

There's something interesting I've noticed which is based on my many interactions with clients over the years as well as from personal observations of people in general, and it's this – the thought of our own individual death tends not to concern us as much as the thought of our loved ones dying. For most of the people I see presenting with anxiety, when discussing their top five fears, the number one fear is almost always illness or accidents resulting in the death of those they love most (usually their partner, children, parents or other close family members). These people tend to feel more emotional about the possible death of a loved one because of the loss it would incur in their lives rather than having any strong fear about their own individual death or where they might go after death. It is certainly how I feel, and after discussing this with many others outside of the therapy context, the general opinion is the same. It seems in many ways that love for others is the far more powerful emotion than fear around our exit from life.

If love is the most powerful of human emotions, what is it that drives the people of one nation to hate and kill people from other nations? Maybe at some stage in the past, something or someone who was well-loved came to great harm due to the action of 'others'. Whether it be tribes, clans, communities or a whole race, when one group of people find it hard to forget the way their loved ones were brutalised by others, that hatred and anger can continue throughout the generations.

Looking back in history, there are few nations that have not been guilty of performing barbaric acts upon others. However, nothing in the past can be changed, only accepted. If perpetrators of crimes can be punished, well and good, but once generations have come and gone, violent incidents of the past belong in the history books, not in our hearts.

For those with a belief in a higher power, it may be easier to let past wrongs go, as revenge belongs to God. It's the same for those who believe in Karma (the belief that what you put out will eventually come back to you). Such beliefs help victims to feel assured that a day of reckoning will surely come, when the villains finally get their comeuppance. Whether true or not, there would certainly be some emotional benefits for victims to think in this way rather than holding onto anger, a sense of power-lessness and injustice.

In the Ideal World

Despite all the wickedness in the world, I believe that people are generally more good than bad. Indeed, it's well known that caring for others can bring a sense of happiness and meaning to life. Studies looking at older people have shown that those who continue to care for someone or something (even pets or plants) tend to fare better both physically and mentally than those who don't. Looking after and pleasing each other seems to be a natural instinct. As well as being a product of learned behaviour, we are biologically geared towards nurturing and being respon-sible for others in our families or communities (our tribes), and obviously there is good survival value in this. Given this biological predisposition towards nurturing and caring about the welfare of others, it might be true to say that we humans generally have a huge capacity to love more than we have a desire to murder and create pain and suffering for others.

Being somewhat idealistic at times, it's easy to overlook the more brutal aspects of the natural world. It could be claimed that emotional concepts such as compassion, fairness and sympathy don't actually exist outside the human realm, and that we developed these qualities as part of our evolutionary progression towards innate goodness, civilisation and survival.

Even while enchanted by the natural beauty of what I see from my deck at home, I'm also aware that under the sea and in the ground, and in the trees all around me, there is a continuous life and death struggle going on. The heron is taking away the life of fish while the other birds are taking life away from insects, all of which reminds me of Tennyson's description of nature being "red in tooth and claw" from his poem *In Memoriam*.

Kindness, compassion or fairness wouldn't make sense in an environment where creatures stalk and kill other creatures in order to survive. But in our human environment, fostering these civilising attributes does make sense, as they help to build a more ethical social environment, and therefore a happier world for the human race.

In my time, I am fortunate to have come across individuals who could be described as being 'highly evolved' in that they are civilised in the truest sense of the word. On the other hand, there are people who are more savage than the wildest of beasts, but luckily for us, they are few and far between. Most of us are somewhere in the middle of these two extremes, but definitely (in my opinion anyway) leaning more towards the good end of the scale.

I often wonder what it would be like if *all* humans were to place kindness to others as the most important *raison d'etre*. Just imagine it, there would be no need to spend vast amounts of money on weaponry or armed forces to defend our countries as nobody would be attacking. Crime would be non-existent. Problems such as disease and hunger would be tackled on a global scale because we would all be caring for each other. It would certainly solve most of the world's problems. Imagining such a situation brings to mind the words from the Beatles' song 'All You Need is Love' and John Lennon's 'Imagine'. Idealistic thinking, of course, but if we ever reach that advanced state, any highly evolved aliens passing by out there might decide – "yes, they are finally ready for a visit!"

Being Kind to Ourselves

When we perform acts of kindness towards others, we feel good. In fact, much of the advice we hear in regard to emotional well-being insists that the path to happiness lies in being of service to others. Although this is certainly a good thing, I believe it's even more important that we direct acts of kindness towards ourselves too. Charity begins at home, and in this case home is the self. In my work I see many unhappy people who don't even like themselves, let alone love themselves.

Developing love and kindness towards ourselves and treating ourselves in a compassionate way doesn't mean becoming narcissistic and self absorbed. It just means psychologically stepping outside of the self, making sure we treat ourselves with the same respect and kindness that we might direct towards others. Sometimes it can be as though we are always at the end of our own kindness queue. If this seems to be the case for you, try seeing what it's like to go to the front of that queue. Think of it being a bit like the instructions we are given prior to taking off in a plane, when you are told to make sure you put on your own oxygen mask before worrying about anybody else. I believe it's important that we nurture ourselves before we can really nurture our fellow human beings. You can call it developing self-esteem if you like, but there's nothing wrong with loving yourself, to enjoy being who you are and being your own best friend, and we can do this while still being kind and compassionate towards others.

Life after Death

If we are spiritually inclined, then we are likely to believe in a soul, and therefore some form of life after death. The Greek philosopher Socrates believed that death could only create one of two scenarios, that either it's an endless sleep – nothingness (as we were before being conceived) – or the migration of the soul to another dimension. In other words, there is something or there is nothing.

Ghosts
There are plenty of people who actually believe in ghosts. They believe in them because they claim to have seen them. If there are such things as ghosts, then this would count as strong evidence

that a type of existence is able to occur after death, which in turn would suggest a higher power being in some form of control to organise such a supernatural process. There are, however, other reasons that may help explain why some people see ghosts or experience unexplainable phenomena and I believe it may have something to do with emotions.

When a person is in the grip of very powerful emotions such as intense grief after losing a loved one, the strength of the emotion may influence how their brain processes what their physical senses are picking up. To provide examples, clients who come to see me suffering from grief often tell me how, within the first few weeks of their partner's death, they start to sense a presence in the house. This may be in the form of a certain smell, sound, sight or touch, or they feel a sudden drop in temperature in some part of a room. As an example, on the Sunday morning two weeks after the death of her husband Jim, Alice came downstairs and noticed a strong smell of fried bacon in the kitchen. She had no bacon in the house, but her deceased husband had always liked bacon for breakfast on Sunday mornings. Alice's house was on a ten-acre block of land so there were no nearby neighbours who might have been frying bacon that morning. To Alice, this could only be a message from Jim letting her know that he was still around and for her not to fret. But could this also have been a case of Alice's disturbed psyche providing her with some well-needed psychological comfort at that time?

Seeing an apparition of the deceased partner standing by the bed at night seems to be the more common example of unexplained phenomena that I hear about. Others have involved photographs suddenly falling off a shelf, the sense of being gently touched on the shoulder or hearing their partner's voice calling their name. If these events really do occur, then they indicate that the deceased have some limited access to the physical world which can be utilised in an effort to reconnect with loved ones. However, given the emotional state of the person who has been left without their life partner, it's possible that by anticipating and intently seeking out 'messages' from the loved one, they are 'finding' them. These messages or signals often provide relief from emotional pain and instil the hope of one day meeting the beloved again on 'the other side'. This obviously provides a tremendous sense of comfort during an emotionally agonising time.

When my sister's husband died recently after a painful illness, she was grief-stricken. But she also felt guilty because of the sense of relief she was experiencing after a harrowing eighteen months of nursing him. One night shortly after his funeral, my sister saw a bright blue light flash across the bedroom ceiling. There was no traffic outside and no explanation could be found for it. She interpreted this as a message that her husband was angry with her for feeling relieved when he finally died. As he was a keen Everton football supporter (this team's colour being blue), she concluded that the light was some sort of message from him. She became too frightened to sleep in the master bedroom in case the 'angry blue light' returned.

While staying with my sister in the UK, I discussed the strange case of the blue light with her. I suggested that if it was him, then that means there is some type of existence after death, so that in itself might be good news compared to there being nothing (for this reason alone, I would love to see a ghost!). I also asked her why he would be angry with her just because she experienced some positive emotion such as relief when his awful physical suffering finally came to an end. Surely if he loved her he would be pleased she had felt some relief and perhaps the blue light represented love rather than anger. I slept in that 'haunted' bedroom throughout my three weeks' visit and never saw anything that could be described as paranormal, but then I wasn't expecting to see anything.

Some people claim to catch a glimpse of their pet waiting at the door at home soon after the same pet's death. Apart from the possibility of intense grief playing with their psyche, this may simply be a case of sensory habit. We get used to seeing or hearing certain everyday things, like the cat at the door, or footsteps on the stairs, or kettles being filled in the kitchen, and we become conditioned to experiencing these sensations as being the norm. After a certain time, new sounds and sights become the sensory routine as our everyday life changes and the old routines disappear.

In discussing the concept of life after death with my husband, we decided that if it was at all possible, whoever of us died first would make some attempt to contact the other. Our pact even involves using a secret little code that only the other person would recognise. An obvious flaw in this plan is the emotional state of the surviving partner. The power of emotion can be so intense, it can influence how we interpret information passing through our five senses, creating something personal from haphazard events and thereby creating special meaning from them.

I remember as a child, the woman who lived across the road lost her five-year-old son in a road accident. She was stricken with grief, spending much of her time crying. Then one day she stopped crying. She told my mum that her little boy had appeared by her bed at night. He was holding some sort of a candle and asked her to stop crying as her tears kept putting out his light. He assured her that he was okay and had been playing with other children in heaven, but they all had bright lights when they went to bed and he didn't. The boy then disappeared. Imagine the sense of comfort that grieving mother must have gained from her child's 'visitation'.

It was when thinking about this and other similar stories that I began to wonder if there is something in the human psyche that tries to help out when we are in enormous emotional pain by creating comforting visions, sounds, sensations, dreams or even smells in order for us to continue functioning in life. Alternatively, the little boy really was in another dimension playing with other children in heaven which, of course, is a very comforting thought as it suggests there is the chance of seeing again the people we dearly love.

Reincarnation

To give some meaning to the great mysteries around life and death, there is the belief of reincarnation. No doubt it feels better emotionally for many people to believe that they will be reborn after death in the form of someone or something else, rather than the thought of no continuation of life at all.

When preparing an assessment for my clients, I often ask them if they have any spiritual beliefs, as from my point of view, for therapy to be successful, knowing a person's spiritual or religious leaning is important. When clients discuss reincarnation, their belief in this is often based on a 'feeling' that it's true rather than being derived from any specific dogma or personal incident. As with most faiths, a belief in reincarnation can provide emotional comfort and the hope of one day meeting up again with loved ones.

Some years ago I was walking through the local Animal Rescue Centre searching for a new pet. I knew that most of the dogs I was looking at were on Death Row and unless somebody claimed or adopted them, they would soon be 'put to sleep'. As I walked along past the cages my heart grew heavier with each step. There was a variety of unwanted dogs, some only just out of their puppyhoods, their tails wagging excitedly as I looked at them. Although it was very difficult, I eventually did choose my new dog. Later that day, I took home Casey, a scruffy little terrier-cross. And like many homeless dogs, Casey turned out to be a very grateful, loving and loyal pet.

You may wonder what all this has to do with reincarnation. While at the Animal Rescue Centre that day, I had a conversation with one of the attendants. I asked her how she managed to work in such a place, seeing beautiful unwanted dogs being 'put down' on a daily basis. She smiled and answered without any hesitation "Oh, they'll all be back!" This woman believed strongly in reincarnation and had no doubt that those dogs being euthanized each day would soon be back in a different body. I thought about her words for a long time, and could only conclude that given her job, to have such a belief might be the only way to cope at an emotional level.

When listening to people discussing reincarnation (both inside and outside of the therapy context), it's interesting to note how often the 'past life' seems to have been something of a prestigious nature. For example, ancient royalty, great warriors or famous historical figures seem to be fairly common. Few, if any, seem to remember a past life when they were a peasant, yet peasants would have been far more plentiful than ancient queens or murdered cardinals. And nobody so far (that I'm aware of) has ever claimed to remember a previous life when they were an ant, a fly or a bacterial organism – life forms even more plentiful than peasants!

If reincarnation is true, then there must be some higher power examining our 'files' and deciding who returns to where and in what form. When people are prepared to accept grinding poverty and suffering because they believe they are being tested, and that their next incarnation is based on how well they endure in this life, then you could say there's a negative aspect to a belief in reincarnation as it's unlikely to encourage activity towards societal change.

Could it be that reincarnation, like all other supernatural beliefs, is something we humans have created for our own emotional comfort in the face of inevitable death, something to satisfy a need for meaning in a mysterious and perhaps meaningless world? Or is it a fact, a reality? Being an agnostic, I can only say I might have my suspicions, but I really don't know.

Cryonics

If you want some chance of living again after your death, but prefer not to pin your hopes on any supernatural beliefs, there is now cryonics. With the help of modern technology, some people are organising to have their bodies frozen when they die in the hope of being brought back to life in the future by the medical scientists who will be alive then. This process is called cryonics and some people are paying lots of money to be preserved at very low temperatures once they die. As medical technology continues to progress at a fast rate, these people assume that by the time they can be brought back to life (maybe in a hundred or two hundred years time) there will be so much extra knowledge and so many technological advancements in medicine that their dead bodies will not only be brought back to life but they will also be made healthy again.

Although this may sound like a good way of ensuring a future resurrection, there are those who take the view that nobody in the future generations would be interested in the revivification of thousands of frozen corpses from the past. I'm not sure I agree, because if we had preserved bodies from the 18th century today, and we had the technology to resurrect them, I believe it would be fascinating to meet up with these people. It would also be fascinating for them to see how we live today in the 21st century. Imagine the composer Mozart finding out that his music has thrived for hundreds of years after his death in 1791, music that has brought joy to millions and is still being played all around the world today. Or imagine if the artist Vincent van Gogh could return and see his paintings now hanging in prestigious art galleries, admired by millions of people all around the world. Even if these great masters were to return for just one day, they would probably be amazed at their level of eminence in the world of music and art. And how marvellous it would be for the lucky people whose task it would be to greet them as they came back to life and enlighten them of their world acclaim! Unfortunately, the remains of Mozart and van Gogh are probably well beyond revivification, but we could say that their immortality has been granted via the great works they have left for future generations to enjoy.

Wherever we go after death, it's likely to be the same place we were before being conceived. We may return to some divine home or return to a state of nothingness, the body being like a light bulb that has burnt out, all the energy has gone and the empty glass bulb is left to eventually return to stardust. Whatever the truth may be, whether we are merely biological accidents of the evolutionary process, the handiwork of a supreme creator, or something else altogether, one thing is important – we need to embrace the fact that right now we are actually 'here'. We could start by looking after our home, our beautiful planet Earth, and imagine how easier it would be to enjoy our time being alive if we *all* placed a high value on treating our fellow humans with respect and kindness. Am I a dreamer? Probably. But I believe it's a dream worth striving for.

Chapter Twelve

Practical Skills for
Maintaining Emotional Well-Being

So far we have looked at how we can optimise our level of happiness by seeking out positive emotional experiences via activities, meditation and mindfulness while simultaneously minimising negative emotional responses via cognitive reframing. There are however, some practical aspects you may also need to consider such as self-care, creating a new routine and how to achieve what you want in life, all of which are covered in this chapter.

Self-Care

As mentioned in Chapter Eight, you don't just have a body, you *are* your body. If you can't quite accept this, then you might prefer to see yourself as being the caretaker of this wonderful machine called your body. Caring for your body involves among other things, nutrition, physical exercise, relaxation and good quality sleep. Self-care also involves being assertive enough with others so that you don't place your body's well-being in jeopardy. At work, this might involve not working too many long hours or taking action by speaking up if something is causing you to feel overly stressed. Being able to say no and to make requests of others is also part of having a healthy regard for your mental and physical health. How often do we hear of people dying before they even reach retirement age, failing to put their own well-being first as they worked themselves into an unhealthy state for the sake of an uncaring and indifferent company? Your precious body is worth far more than this.

Being a Good Caretaker of Your Body

If you are obese or stick insect thin, then you are probably not a good caretaker of your body. You need to be on your body's side, it carries out amazing things all day and night for you, working hard to keep you alive. The least you can do to help is to treat it with respect by maintaining a healthy diet.

Eating is a pleasurable experience and enjoying food is one of the most natural things in the world. Nature intended it that way to ensure our survival. But we have choices regarding what we eat. Eating healthily simply means eating a variety of good foods as part of our everyday routine, not too much, not too little. This routine is what creates 'lifestyle'. There are plenty of books available on what constitutes a healthy diet, so I won't go into that here.

I don't believe that enjoying small indulgences now and again is a bad thing. In fact, being able to experience some pleasurable feelings from small luxuries is better than a Spartan life of self-denial. We are, after all, here to enjoy ourselves! However, the key word really is *moderation*, which means now and again. If it's a regular indulgence, then it's not moderation and could be more harmful than helpful. It's what we do on a regular basis that determines the quality of our lifestyle not what we sometimes do.

If you smoke, take recreational drugs or over-indulge in alcohol on a regular basis, then you are definitely not being a good caretaker of your body. There are better, safer ways to feel good than plying your body with harmful toxic substances. Your precious body really does deserve better than this.

Regular Physical Exercise

Our bodies were never meant to be sitting down at a desk or watching TV for long periods of time, and if your life is like this, then you might want to ensure that physical activity is a top priority for you. There are those who love going to the gym to do physical exercise while others loathe such places. I must admit to not being a lover of hard, full-on exercise. I have tried joining gyms, more than once paying a full year's subscription fee, only to attend three or four times. To me, there's not much in the way of beauty to be found in a gym. I don't like the smell, the music is usually mediocre and some of the exercise equipment resembles torture instruments from medieval times! It all seems such a useless waste of energy – dozens of people walking, cycling, running and rowing, but going nowhere. Regardless of my rather negative description of gyms, physical exercise is important, not only for our physical well-being but also for our mental health. If you feel down or stressed, a bout of physical exercise to get your heart beating fast can be really helpful. As well as being good for increasing the amount of oxygen to the brain, an increased heart rate circulates blood around the body which can help with repair and healing.

As I love and respect my body, I make sure I engage in physical exercise on a regular basis (without going near a gym!). Studies have shown that regular exercise can actually change the brain cells and be mood enhancing. I spend about twenty minutes every second day on an exercise cycle, gaining pleasure from some wonderful music while I pedal. If it wasn't for the music, it would be tediously boring, but the music can often turn it into a delightful experience. Sometimes I climb off the cycle indulging an overwhelming urge to dance rather than pedal. I also make sure I go for a daily walk of about twenty to thirty minutes duration. I walk with my dog down to a reserve at the end of the road and back home again. Being mindful of my body moving along, and being in the precious moment of my life, I make an effort to notice the environment – trees, the sky, flowers and the little kingfisher bird who likes to sit on his usual branch of an old pine tree. I find this far more interesting and fulfilling than being at a sweat-laden gym. And it's entertaining to see my dog zealously sniffing at hedges and tree trunks, no doubt catching up on all the latest canine gossip of the street!

The Importance of Sleep

O gentle sleep! Nature's soft nurse.
William Shakespeare

As well as making sure we eat healthily and engage in regular physical exercise, self-care involves having good quality sleep. For me, falling asleep is one of the most pleasant of experiences and how apt seems Shakespeare's description of "gentle sleep" being "Nature's soft nurse". As most life forms need some type of sleep or rest, there is obviously survival value in sleep. Studies have shown a definite link between our health and our sleep. While we sleep, the body is busy with repair and rejuvenation, which is why many people describe feeling better both physically and emotionally after a good night's sleep.

A recent survey found that 70% of people believe they don't get enough sleep, so sleep is obviously an issue for a lot of people. Many of the people who come to see me for therapy have trouble with sleeping. Some fall asleep easily enough once in bed, but wake up at around 2am with an active mind, whereas others have trouble getting off to sleep. A common worry for those with a sleep-disturbed night is how tired they will be the next day.

As our bodies tend to work best with routines, if you are having problems with sleep, make sure you create some routine around sleeping. Going to bed at the same time each night and rising at the same time each morning (whether you have had a good night's sleep or not) can help your body to become accustomed to a set routine. As it's easy to develop habits, try not to do much of anything other than sleep when you go to bed. Your bed needs to be associated in your brain with sleeping. Sex or light pre-sleep reading can be fine, but everything else such as working on a computer or watching TV is best done in some other room before bedtime.

Some therapists recommend getting up out of bed and doing

something if you can't sleep, for example, watch TV, do some ironing, or read a book. But I believe that if you want to develop a sleeping routine, then it's best to stay in bed. If you regularly get up at 2am to watch TV because you can't get back to sleep, then that's the habit you are training your mind and body to get used to. To my mind, it's far better to practice relaxation exercises to de-activate the mind and stay in your bed.

Some recommendations for a good night's sleep are:

- Make sure your bedroom has adequate fresh air.
- Use cotton sheets rather than sheets made from synthetic materials.
- Don't consume caffeine from 3pm onwards.
- Don't drink alcohol after 8pm (and only drink in moderation).
- Have your evening meal as early as possible.
- Don't do vigorous physical exercise in the evenings.
- Don't read mentally stimulating books or watch exciting or thought provoking films prior to going to sleep. If you like to read before going to sleep, make it fairly low-key reading.
- Engage in a relaxation exercise such as meditation if you have problems falling asleep or returning to sleep.
- Don't catastrophise about not sleeping. For example don't think "This is terrible! I won't be able to function properly at work tomorrow." Fretting about not sleeping is likely to make you anxious, and anxiety is not conducive to being relaxed enough to sleep.
- Turn your clock away from you so you can't monitor the time while you are awake.
- If you have tried all of the above, and really can't sleep, simply experience being in the moment. Enjoy the comfort of the bed, the quiet, the dark, the bliss of being able to just lie there with your eyes closed doing absolutely nothing.

Some people develop fears around being tired. They make themselves anxious about not sleeping, clock-watching for most of the night – "It's now 3am and I'm still not asleep, and I'll be so tired tomorrow, I'll just be a write-off!" How could anybody thinking like this feel relaxed enough to get to sleep? If you are ever in this situation, it's 3am and you haven't yet fallen asleep, it's far better to turn the clock around so the time isn't visible, and think to yourself – "If I am tired tomorrow, it's not the end of the world, and I intend to deal with it to the best of my ability then. Right now, I'm going to start the breathing meditation and know that even if I don't go to sleep, meditating will be a huge benefit to my mental and physical well-being." Chances are by thinking like this and engaging in a basic breathing meditation, you will soon fall asleep.

As well as creating a wonderful sense of relaxation, meditation really is a great tool for closing the mind down and falling off to sleep. As mentioned in Chapter Three, I find that mantra meditation works extremely well for me if I want to sleep. What could be more boring than to have the mind focused on the same word repeated over and over? Is it any wonder that sleep can come so quickly when there is so little mental processing going on? Even counting sheep would require more mental processing than repeating a mantra over and over! Even if meditation doesn't put you to sleep, some gurus assure us that twenty minutes of meditation can be equivalent to a couple of hours of good quality sleep.

You have a choice of mantra meditation (mentally repeating a word) or the basic breathing meditation. Either of these meditation styles can be relaxing enough to drive an active mind into sleep mode. A lot of people want to know how much sleep we actually need each night. Well, there's no exact answer to this question because our individual needs vary, however, some sleep experts suggest that an average of seven and a half hours is a good estimate. You could assess your own optimum number of sleeping hours each night by noticing how refreshed you feel the next morning. Our own bodies usually let us know what is just right for us. Below are a few more lines from the great English bard describing the blessedness of sleep.

Sleep that knits up the ravell'd sleave of care,
The death of each day's life, sore labour's bath,
Balm of hurt minds, great nature's second course,
Chief nourisher in life's feast.
William Shakespeare

Regular Relaxation Exercises

Apart from using meditation to combat insomnia, practicing relaxation exercises on a regular basis can be just as important as regular physical exercise. Yoga has the benefit of combining both physical exercise and relaxation, and many people find that practicing yoga on a regular basis to be invaluable for their sense of well-being.

The mind itself is a useful tool as it provides the means to create whatever 'mind-movie' we want to conjure up in order to help us relax, for example, visual imagery can be used as a type of meditation. Imagine yourself sitting against a tree in a beautiful tranquil country setting, the sun is warm and you are near a gently flowing stream. Try to remain in that mental scene. As soon as a thought about something else intrudes, place the thought on a leaf and let it flow on down the stream and out of sight. As with any meditation style, the idea is to have a means of controlling thoughts so that you can keep coming back to a main mental focus, whether that be sitting against a tree in the imagined country scene, or coming back to a mantra, a candle-flame or your own breathing.

I would advise anybody to really give meditation a good go before quitting it. But if meditation really isn't your choice of relaxation exercise, then you might prefer a completely different one called Progressive Muscle Relaxation. This involves tensing different parts of your body, holding the tension for about ten seconds and then relaxing for about ten seconds. For example, tense your shoulders for ten seconds, then relax them. Then tense your arms, hold the tension, and let them flop in a relaxed state. You repeat this exercise from head to toe with all the different areas of your body. Some people really like this exercise, but it does engage the brain in more mental processing than the meditation exercise does.

Most of us are unaware of how we breathe because it's something that occurs automatically while our focus is elsewhere. But how we breathe makes a difference to how relaxed we feel. When we are anxious or strongly focused, our breathing can become shallow and irregular, we may even hold our breath. An exercise called Abdominal Breathing (also known as Diaphragmatic Breathing or 'belly breathing') is a technique to help us to feel 'centred' and more in control of our body.

To practice the Abdominal Breathing exercise, lie down flat on the floor and place your hands on your abdomen area. When you breathe in, take the breath right down to the bottom of your lungs so that your abdominal area rises rather than your chest. It can help if you imagine having an inflatable ball inside your abdominal area. When you breathe in, the ball inflates, and deflates when you breathe out. Breathing like this ensures that the oxygen reaches the bottom of the lungs which is where the small blood vessels are that carry oxygen through the blood to other areas of the body. This exercise can calm the mind and body and discourages shallow breathing (which can turn into hyper-ventilating if you are anxious).

If you suffer from anxiety, it's better to practice Abdominal Breathing when you aren't anxious rather than to try it for the first time when you are experiencing anxiety symptoms. Once you are confident that you know how to do this breathing exercise, you can do it anywhere, for example, sitting on a bus or walking along the road. Nobody knows that you are breathing deeply like this, and you can begin to feel more relaxed in a matter of seconds.

Practical Problem Solving

We all have problems of one sort or another, in fact, life can often be full of problems. If we want to enjoy our lives and make the most of our precious time here, then we need good problem-solving abilities. Recognising, facing and solving problems all play a role in self-care at a practical level. If we don't know how to go about solving problems, then we are likely to become candidates for stress. For every problem there is usually some solution, and although problems may be difficult, they are rarely insurmountable. Some people do nothing when faced with problems, hoping they will just go away, and sometimes problems do just go away, but for a lot of the time they don't, and without attention of some sort, problems tend to get bigger.

A basic problem solving exercise involves simply following the steps below:

1. Name the problem.
2. Generate options representing possible solutions.
3. Rate each option according to its advantages and disadvantages.
4. Choose the 'best' option according to the above ratings and put it into action.
5. If you find that the option you chose to act upon didn't solve the problem, go back to the beginning and start again using the additional information gained from your initial attempt.
6. If you have given this practical problem solving exercise your best effort and you still can't find a solution to your problem, then discuss it with somebody whose judgement you value.

For much of the time we may be competent at solving problems, but sometimes a situation arises and we are not sure how to go about fixing it. Although the exercise above might appear fairly basic, one of the hardest parts of problem solving is actually naming the problem. Assumptions can easily be made as to what the problem is, but upon a closer examination of the situation we find the real problem is something else all together. Once you have listed the possible solutions, have a good look at each option. Consider all the advantages and disadvantages of each one according to how that particular action is likely to impact on you and others at both an emotional and a practical level. From all your ratings, there is usually one option that will stand out as being the 'best'. This represents your solution (for now). It's good for you to try and solve problems yourself before seeking help from somebody else as this will provide you with experience in problem solving, which after all, is just a normal part of life.

Sometimes the problem can involve really hating your job. We mostly work because we need money to live as well as to help us achieve goals such as buying a house or a car. The sad part of somebody hating their job is that most of their precious time is spent preferring to be somewhere else other than being where they are. If you are in this situation, take some time out to problem solve, to consider what your options for change might be. All those hours, days, months and years represent your life and it's up to you to make sure you enjoy your time on Earth as much as possible, rather than spend it wishing you were somewhere else. I'm not suggesting that you walk out of a job you don't like (although you could do this depending on your financial circumstances and career goals), but you could start planning an 'escape route'. This might involve looking at finding another job, self-employment, training for some other type of work, moving to another city or country or seeking a transfer to a different department within the same company. Once you have an escape plan, you can start viewing the undesirable job as your temporary job rather than as your permanent job. It's far easier to tolerate 'suffering' when we know it's of a short-term duration than when it's something more permanent.

Creating a New Routine

We all tend to have some sort of routine in our everyday lives, and it's our routine that develops both the wanted and unwanted habits. When bad habits develop, we can feel annoyed with ourselves, recognising that this is not what we want, but at the same time finding it difficult to initiate change towards what we do want. So let's look at some strategies that can help when this happens.

Overcoming Procrastination

One of the first obstacles to be overcome when wanting to change something is procrastination. Procrastination is when we find it hard to get going on a task that needs to be done, continually making excuses to postpone it until some better time in the future. We can beat ourselves up emotionally because we want to get started, yet a lack of motivation causes us to keep putting it off. If it's a task that is likely to require quite a bit of time to complete (for example, sorting out a shed full of stuff or completing a university assignment), a sense of feeling overwhelmed may stop us from even starting the task. And the longer we keep putting it off, the worse we feel about ourselves. For people who are depressed, even completing a small task such as going shopping or making something to eat can seem too much to cope with.

If you are a procrastinator, there are strategies that can help you overcome this, for example, the 'Just do it!' statement. Whatever negative thinking style is conjured up to discourage you from even starting on a task – "I'll do it tomorrow when I'll have more energy" or "I'm too tired right now" or "I just couldn't be bothered" – try challenging these thoughts by stating very firmly to yourself "Regardless of how you *feel*, just do it!" Then you have a good chance of actually getting started on the task. Take your tiredness, your lethargy and your negativity with you and just begin the job anyway. The secret of overcoming procrastination is to simply get started on the task. Motivation tends to follow action. You could sit there waiting a long time for motivation to come and energise you when it is any initial movement towards the task that's needed.

Another useful strategy for overcoming procrastination, especially when it's a big task that needs to be tackled, is called the Swiss Cheese technique (Swiss cheese is the cheese with lots of holes in it). To use this cheese analogy, imagine you are going to make a hole in your task by taking a small bite out of it. So let's say you want to tidy up the shed, you could simply think to yourself "I'm only going to work on tidying up the far left corner, and that will be my lot for the day." But as motivation follows action, once you have completed tidying that far left corner, that's when you are likely to feel motivated to continue with just another 'small bite' while you are up and about. Perhaps the right hand corner of the shed may be the next small job, and so on.

For the Swiss Cheese technique, you can also use time rather than a designated part of a task. For example, to help you to get going on a university assignment, you could say to yourself that you will just get out all the information about what needs to be done, and read it for only thirty minutes. That is your small bite. But after thirty minutes, rather than put it all away, it's likely you will want to continue for a bit longer while you are starting to work out what needs to be done next.

There are other strategies that can help you get going despite a sluggish mood. If you whip yourself up into a guilt-ridden state with *should* statements – "I should start this now" – but nothing happens, you can challenge and reframe the thought by saying to yourself – "There's no rule in the universe dictating that I should start this task now, but I'm choosing to start it even though I don't feel like doing it." Thinking more like this reduces the pressure you put on yourself to act, and ironically, it places you with more control to take action.

I know from past experiences that, for me, tedious repetitious jobs involving housework can result in procrastination. Although some people enjoy cleaning their home, getting stuck in with enthusiasm, for others this type of activity can be mind-numbingly boring. In my case, the monotony of jobs such as cleaning windows or washing floors is overcome by simply putting on the type of music that I love to move to, especially Latin American music. This immediately transforms the most monotonous of housework chores into an enjoyable and happy event.

When trying to overcome procrastination, it's useful to remember how good that sense of achievement feels when you finally complete the task you have been putting off, the sense of taking some control back and feeling your spirits lift and your body energised. It's well worth breaking off the chains of procrastination in order to experience this.

Changing Habits

To rid ourselves of unwanted habits, there are two ways in which we can achieve this. We can either organise a gradual change or we can make an immediate change and try to maintain it as the new status quo. In my experience the gradual change works better than going for an abrupt instant conversion, especially if you are trying to make lifestyle changes such as eating more healthily or adding exercise to your daily routine.

Let's say you want to change your eating habits so that eating healthily is part of your new lifestyle goals. One of the best ways to do this is to begin by changing just one of your main meals – breakfast, lunch or dinner. Choose one of these mealtimes and put all your energy and focus into changing and maintaining this to fit your new healthy regime.

Let's say you choose to change how you eat breakfast. Consider what you want to be the new healthy breakfast that you would like to maintain, and only eat that each day for breakfast. If you can keep this up for about a month, it's likely to become established as your new breakfast habit. Remember that we humans are geared towards cultivating habits, so try to make it easy for yourself by just changing one thing at a time.

When the new breakfast habit is formed (usually after four weeks of keeping to it), then you can start to change your lunch habits too by using the same process. Then once the habit of eating healthy breakfasts and lunches is established, you will probably feel quite motivated to tackle changing the final mealtime routine. Before long, eating a healthy dinner will also become the norm, resulting in the achievement of your goal within three months. You can use this same principle to eliminate unhealthy snacking between main meals if that is a problem for you.

The key factor when making lifestyle changes is the gradual development of new habits. Once a habit is formed, it becomes the norm, the new routine that just rolls along of its own accord without you having to control or monitor it. This is why trying to change all aspects of your lifestyle simultaneously can be doomed to failure. Well-known American writer Mark Twain summed it up nicely – "Old habits can't be thrown out of an upstairs window. They have to be coaxed down the stairs one step at a time."

Scheduling Pleasurable Activities
We all have twenty-four hours in each of our days, and how we spend those hours will obviously vary according to our circumstances. However, if you don't have *any* time in your day when you are experiencing some real pleasure, then your life is probably out of balance. It's so easy for us to become caught up with work or unhelpful time-wasting pursuits that bring little in

the way of happiness, leaving very few opportunities for us to truly savour our lives on a daily basis. If you are somebody who really enjoys your job, then you will be gaining a lot of pleasure from that source. However, it's still possible that your life is out of balance if you are so engrossed in your work that you are missing out on other experiences.

Before scheduling activities into your life, it's helpful to know what types of things bring you happiness. If you aren't sure, think about the times when you really felt happy and make a note of what you were doing then. You could also try engaging in some new activities. By being more spontaneous and open to trying new things, you are likely to discover the types of activities that bring you positive emotional experiences as well as those that don't.

If you really can't find time to organise pleasurable activities for yourself, see what it's like to be mindful of all that you do throughout your day – eating, walking, driving, what you see, hear, taste, smell or touch. It may surprise you to find that pleasure, as well as a sense of awe and wonder, can be gained from the little everyday things that we fail to appreciate in our rush to get on with more 'work'.

When we live each day in the full knowledge that we are privileged players in this great theatre of life, a psychological shift takes place in how we view each of the hours in our days. This makes it easier to ensure we live life to the full, whatever that might mean for each one of us given our unique personalities and circumstances.

Achieving What You Want in Life

You are today where the thoughts of yesterday have brought you and you will be tomorrow where the thoughts of today take you.
Blaise Pascal

In order to have what you want in life, you need to be able to name it. What we want often changes according to the different stages of our life, for example, when we are young, our goals can be quite different to what we want later on. Right now, whatever age you are, could you name what it is that you want to achieve? And even if you do know what you want, do you know how you will go about achieving it?

Setting and Achieving Goals

Most of us have ideas about what we want, but how many of us start each New Year's Day with a list of goals we want to achieve that year, many of which never come to fruition? Goals need to be short-term, medium-term and long-term. Obviously a long-term goal such as completing a PhD at university cannot be achieved by the end of the year, but a short-term goal in relation to such a big goal might be to talk to a professor at university in regard to supervision for a PhD. If you don't know what you want in life, have a good think, and start with the bigger, longer term goals. Then when you make your short-term or medium-term goals, they can be part of those bigger aspirations.

As an example of goal-setting, let's say your long-term goal is to own your own house, but you know that over the next twelve months (even when saving as much as you can) you won't have enough money even for a deposit. In this case, a short-term goal could be to open a savings account (maybe one offering a good interest rate) that will help with your savings. The medium-term goal will be to save enough money for a deposit on a house, still leaving the long-term goal to own that house as an ongoing objective.

Many of you will have come across the well known acronym SMART used for practical goal-setting. These letters represent:

Specific (Name exactly what the goal is).
Measurable (You need to know how to measure the steps

involved towards achieving the goal).

Achievable (The goal needs to be in the realms of possibility).

Relevant (Is this something that is worth your while achieving?).

Timely (Goals need timeframes so you need to have some idea when this goal will be achieved).

As an example of how I go about setting and achieving goals, the first week in each January I start with my list of what I would like to achieve during the next twelve months. I have stopped writing *Get fit and lose weight* on my list as I believe my everyday general lifestyle will automatically look after this, so there's no need to fret about what I weigh or to look at joining a gym.

On my list I have three categories. In the first category I have all the small things I want. Examples on this list might be buying a new black skirt (if I needed one). The second category I call Home and Beauty and below this title I write down all the things I want to buy or do that will enhance the beauty of the home. Examples might be to put a new plant on the deck, paint the ceiling in the kitchen or remove all the rubbish that has accumulated by the compost bin. This is the list that I share with my husband as most of the items on the list are jobs around the house and garden for him! Although he might groan looking at it, I strongly suspect he gains a lot of pleasure from achieving these practical tasks, and it's good that I can help him to increase his level of happiness in this way!

The third goal list contains what I call my personal aspirations. They are often the *What I want to do before I die* type of goals, and I write down only those that I aim to do by the end of that year. Some type of holiday is usually on this list, and as my family are scattered all over the world, the holiday usually combines seeing family members. Another goal on this list might be to learn something new, for example, a different style of cooking, a new language or even signing up for a course of ballroom dancing or painting. Sometimes it may be to attend a certain conference or workshop that will enhance my work as a psychologist. Life is so full of different things to experience, yet we have such a limited amount of time, even if we live to one hundred years old, it wouldn't cover a fraction of the time needed to cover the variety of activities available. This is why I find my lists very helpful.

So at the beginning of each year, I create my three lists. By the end of the year, most of the goals on those lists have been achieved, with a big tick next to each one. Anything that is not achieved is put on the following year's list if it's still a goal. I don't beat myself up emotionally if goals aren't achieved by the end of the year. To my mind, a goal list is a guide that reminds us of what we want out of life that year, and it's with a great sense of achievement that goals (both small and big) are crossed off the list as they are completed. The goal list is never allowed to become the dictator, it's simply a guide. You are always in charge of your goal list.

If you really don't know what you want in life, then you may end up being at the mercy of whatever happens to come your way. Like a 'candle in the wind', you will go whichever way the wind blows rather than the direction you might prefer to go. It's possible you could be a very laid-back type of person and simply enjoy whatever comes your way. However, if you prefer to place some control on how your life is spent, setting goals can be helpful. If you don't set yourself goals, later on you could end up regretting how you wasted your precious opportunity to really experience life. Planning how you will achieve future goals can still be done in the present moment. You are not living in the future but being in the moment as you work out what you want in life and how you aim to go about getting it.

To help you generate ideas about what you would like to achieve, try experimenting with the following approach. Imagine your adult life in its three main stages – youth, middle-age and elderly. What sorts of things would you like to experience or have in your current and future stages of life? When I was young, I wanted to travel, to see what it was like to have holidays overseas. I wanted to get married, buy a house and have babies. I achieved all these things before the age of twenty-five but not in the way I had envisaged. Emigrating to New Zealand was not on my goal list, neither was leaving my young children in day care centres all day while I worked full-time to earn money. As my fellow Liverpudlian, John Lennon, reminds us in one of his songs – Life is what happens to you while you're busy making other plans. That, of course is true, but some ideas about what you want in life are better than none at all. Goals associated with enjoying our precious bit of time on Earth are probably the most important of all.

Whatever you can do, or dream you can, begin it. Boldness
has genius, power, and magic in it. Begin it now.
Johann Wolfgang von Goethe

Being Authentic

There's a type of lizard known as a chameleon, a creature which is able to change its colour to fit in with different natural environments. There are also people (commonly referred to as social chameleons) who change their personalities to fit in with whatever their social setting happens to be at the time. We might all do this now and again to some extent, but if you do it most of the time, you might need to ask yourself if you are really living *your* life the way *you* want to?

I was recently at a social event held in an up-market venue in the city when I came across a sight that almost made me laugh out loud. As I was observing a group of about eight to ten young men (probably aged in their late twenties or early thirties), I noticed they all had exactly the same hairstyles (moussed up at the front). Although this in itself wasn't too surprising given the power of fashion trends, these young men were all holding an opened beer bottle (all the same brand) in their right hand, and were intermittently swigging at the bottle as though they were babies with their milk bottles. But the similarities went further than that. As they stood in a circle chatting and swigging, I noticed that every one of them had their left hand in their left trouser pocket and were standing in exactly the same way (legs slightly apart). It was as though I had stumbled across some tightly choreographed comedy act!

I wondered if there was anyone in that group being their authentic self. To me, this looked like strict conformity to the social herd. Being a psychologist, I can understand why people want to fit in by being similar to each other. A need to be accepted based on similarity makes sense as the safety of the herd is very appealing. It takes courage to be different, to drink your favourite brand of beer from a glass or not drink beer at all, or to have your hair the way you want to wear it regardless of the current fashion.

Although wanting to fit in is understandable, the failure to live an authentic life can become an issue of deep regret later on down the years. A friend of mine who has worked in a hospice for many years told me that one of the most common regrets expressed by people who are dying is that they didn't live an authentic life. They wished they had been more selfish, less concerned with what others think and less frightened of change or being different. They mourned the fact that they had lived their lives according to how others expected them to be rather than how they themselves would like to have been. Most of the dreams and hopes they once had in their younger days (the small as well as the big dreams) were never realised as they became caught up with 'fitting in' and just plodding along on the treadmill of life until physical decline and illness removed all opportunities for change.

Looking at your life right now, how authentic does it appear?

When we realise from both an emotional and an intellectual perspective just how precious and how fleeting life actually is, it becomes easier to be your true self, and how much better to realise this sooner rather than when it's too late.

The privilege of a lifetime is to become who you truly are.
Carl Jung

Chapter Thirteen

Gaining the Larger Perspective

Now that we are nearing the end of the book, in this final chapter I want to emphasise the importance of emotionally and intellectually embracing the Big Picture concepts – birth, death, and the all important bit in between (all the days of our lives). This larger perspective really does provide a valuable framework for all that's been covered in the book so far. Reading this last chapter could just be the catalyst you still need to begin actively managing your emotions in order to make the most of your precious time on Earth.

Between the Immensities

As a child growing up in Liverpool, my mother would push a pram to the local shops, accompanied by her three young children. I was the eldest of the three girls, and when my mother stopped to talk with the other mothers (who were also pushing prams accompanied by a variety of children), I liked to listen closely to their adult conversations. Even from a young age, I was fascinated by how these women interacted with each other. There were bits of local news about various goings on, a lot of facial expressions to accentuate certain aspects of this news and plenty of gesticulation. Rather than being interested in the other children around me, I studied the mothers, focusing intently on their interactions.

On meeting, the first question these women often asked each other in their broad Liverpool accents was "How are you keeping Love?" (everyone seemed to be called Love which I suppose helped to avoid problems with forgetting names). It was my mother's occasional reply to this question that I particularly remember. With a sigh, she would say "Oh, you know, still struggling between the immensities." Like many Liverpudlians, my mother's background was Irish, and she would sometimes use this old Irish phrase when asked how she was doing. The immensities are birth and death, the bit in between is life. As well as being referred to as the immensities, birth and death were also known as 'the mysteries'. Although my mother had a Christian upbringing, she always claimed that none of us really know what life is all about. Terms such as *immensities* and *mysteries* held a certain hint of excitement, but the *struggling* bit used to describe everyday adult life left me with a vague apprehension about growing up and having to face the inevitable hard times ahead.

When thinking about the idea of life being a struggle, if we look within the larger context, the real struggle for life began a very long time ago. Without the right environmental conditions on our planet, we humans wouldn't even exist. Whether you believe a divine creator, evolution or something else is responsible for human life on Earth, it's important to acknowledge that for a very long time there have been huge struggles for survival taking place on our planet. Without speculating on the complexities of what may have been going on billions of years ago, it's useful to simply keep in mind the extraordinary hardships that our early ancestors must have suffered. To survive through famine, drought, disease, severe heat and cold without any of the basic requisites that we take for granted today would require real endurance. The bubonic plague alone killed a third of the population of Europe in just five years during the 14th century, and of course, there must have been many adversities suffered that we remain unaware of.

Charles Darwin, the 19th century English naturalist associated with the theory of evolution referred to this struggle for survival as 'natural selection', which was later termed 'the survival of the fittest' by philosopher Herbert Spencer. And it was *our* ancestors who did survive, making it possible for us to be here today. Their endurance enabled our current existence. Even going back a mere 300 years to 18th-century Europe, the infant mortality rate was as high as 50%, meaning that only one out of two living babies born would reach their first birthday. We are the descendants of children who did survive, so when we consider the gigantic struggle for human life to survive on Earth, it's important to remember that we are part of all who have gone before.

The Great Race for Life

Continuing with the concept of life as a struggle, let's think about what happens at conception. Going back to the very beginning of your individual human existence, when the particular sperm that represented half of you proved fast enough and strong enough to be the first to reach and fertilise the second part of you (the egg), that was when you won the most important, the biggest race of all, the race for life! You won the opportunity to experience being a human being on planet Earth.

Do any of us really have a full appreciation of this prize that has been won? Anyone taking a gamble, for example, buying a lotto ticket or having a bet on a horse, often has an interest in the odds of their winning. In the race for life, the odds of an individual sperm reaching an egg are not hundreds or thousands to one, but millions to one. In other words, there were millions of competitors racing for that chance at life as a human being, and YOU won. The sperm that represented you got to the egg before all the others. This was the very beginning of your life. Your father's sperm and your mother's egg developed into you, so right away, and at a very individual level, you won a gigantic struggle for a chance at existence.

When I watch documentaries on TV about how a human baby develops in the mother's womb, it never fails to leave me feeling awe-inspired. A brand new life coming into the world really is an immense concept. The struggle for birth is at one end of the phenomenon we call life, and at the other end is death.

Our Inevitable Departure

If you are ever lucky enough to travel to Rome, there's an interesting tourist attraction known as the Capuchin Crypt. It's located under a church called the Santa Maria della Concezione. This crypt provides an elaborate display of bones belonging to over 4,000 Capuchin monks who lived between 1528 and 1870. The message on a plaque in the crypt warns us – *What you are now, we once were; what we are now, you shall be.* Although this may seem macabre, it's a strong reminder of how transient our lives are.

Maintaining an awareness of our inevitable departure can have an immense impact on how we live. For example, when we become caught up in the petty dramas of everyday life, we completely forget the transient nature of our existence, the value of each hour of each day. Death is a sobering thought, but an important one if we are to make the most of this great prize we have each won.

You have probably heard the saying *carpe diem*, meaning 'seize the day'. To do that, you need to treasure the present moment. To have the realisation that one day, you and all your contemporaries will no longer be here makes it important that you fully experience being alive now. Death represents the other immensity, and is a concept we need to intellectually and emotionally embrace. When you think about the fact that we are born, we live a certain number of days and then we die, it really is a mysterious business and certainly an immense concept for our human minds to take in.

As a child, I remember a time when I believed in miracles. At Sunday school, the teachers told us that God would perform miracles if we prayed long and hard enough and only if we really believed. One day, when I was about eight years old, while walking home from school, I came across a dead pigeon in the road. Picking the bird up, I carefully observed its cold dead form, the head dangling limply, the red-rimmed eyes open and staring but seeing nothing. I put its body inside my coat and took it home. Without telling anybody what I was doing, I gently wrapped the dead pigeon in tissue paper and placed it in the deepest drawer in my parent's bedroom, concealing the parcel underneath my father's work socks.

Over the next few days I prayed to God for the pigeon to return to life. I assumed that God would probably expect at least a week of steadfast prayer as proof of my absolute faith before performing any miracles. In seven days' time I intended to open the bedroom window wide, pull out the drawer and let the resurrected pigeon fly away, no doubt to the accompaniment of a heavenly choir! But I never got to see any miracles. Nobody told me that dead things start to decompose and stink, and when my parents eventually discovered the source of the stench in their bedroom, I had to tell them all about the miracle I was trying to organise. In no uncertain terms I was ordered to take the bird's rotting corpse (a harbinger of Bad Luck if ever there was one) out of the house and organise my miracles somewhere else!

The pigeon incident was my first experience with death. As I grew up I became less naïve about the demise of living creatures, and when at the age of twelve I came across the stiff little body of my pet kitten accidentally drowned in a bucket of water, I realised the cruel indifference and totality of death. We, like all living creatures, are just 'passing through' and it's the transient nature of our existence that makes the life we have right now all the more valuable. In view of this, enjoying our experience of being alive is of paramount importance.

The Bit In Between

Between the immensities of birth and death are all the days of our lives. A common piece of advice from those approaching the end of their existence on Earth is that we should make more effort to simply enjoy ourselves while we are here, to make the most of it. In line with this advice, the Buddhist philosophy claims that we are all here to enjoy ourselves and to do no harm to others in the process.

It's with good reason that the famous lines below from Shakespeare's play *Macbeth* (Act 5, Scene 5) are framed and placed in a prominent position on my desk at home. Read them carefully, and preferably aloud.

Tomorrow, and tomorrow, and tomorrow,
Creeps in this petty pace from day to day,
To the last syllable of recorded time;
And all our yesterdays have lighted fools
The way to dusty death. Out, out, brief candle!
Life's but a walking shadow, a poor player
That struts and frets his hour upon the stage
And then is heard no more. It is a tale
Told by an idiot, full of sound and fury
Signifying nothing.

These words were written over four hundred years ago, yet they still provide that valuable perspective that can prevent us from becoming caught up in the petty dramas of everyday life. Using the power of language, Shakespeare captures the transient nature of our existence. Although the message is hardly joyful, it's a strong reminder of how our precious time can be frittered away on superficial trivia, helping us to mentally step outside ourselves to view life from a much larger standpoint. Throughout much of my adult life, if ever I felt nervous about an uncomfortable situation that was about to come my way, I would read these lines from Macbeth aloud. Almost immediately, I was able to move from the smaller to the larger perspective, and by doing this, any feelings of nervous apprehension were alleviated. To my mind, having this larger perspective of life makes it easier to really experience our moment-by-moment existence.

Many Roads Lead to Rome

As many roads lead to Rome, so there are many ways in which you can enhance your experience of each day. As covered early on in this book, an excellent way to go about enjoying your time here is to seek out and engage in those activities that are able to provide you with positive heart-lifting emotions. Simultaneously, minimise negative emotions by restructuring faulty unhelpful thinking so that you take the more balanced view of a situation. If you can focus working in these two areas, then life will start to become considerably happier. I know this from my work with thousands of people as well as from my own personal experiences.

It's also important that you don't underestimate the power of regular meditation and mindfulness to generate valuable emotions, as well as being authentic in your relationships with others, all of which contribute to your overall enjoyment of life.

Finally, to live your life as fully as you possibly can, take heed of the message that weaves its way throughout this book. Going about your daily life with the Big Picture concept as the backdrop creates a powerful shift in your perception. This shift enables you to greet each new day with a sense of awe and wonder, making it easier to really make the most of this precious opportunity you have to exist for a short time as a human being on our beautiful planet. Appreciate and recognise this special journey as being the wonderful and mysterious adventure it is. Savour every moment while it lasts.

It is only when we truly know and understand that we have a limited time on Earth and that we have no way of knowing when our time is up that we will begin to live each day to the fullest, as if it were the only one we had.
Dr Elisabeth Kubler-Ross

PSYCHE BOOKS

The study of the mind: interactions, behaviours, functions. Developing and learning our understanding of self. Psyche Books cover all aspects of psychology and matters relating to the head.